being in the world

 A is for alphabets & apples

 B is for bags & brushes

 C is for collections & colourful curriculum

 D is for doors

 E is for enemies

 F is for furniture

  G is for goats, goldfish, guinea pigs & other gorgeous animals

H is for homes

 acting on the world

Z is for zigzag through the book

Y is for yesterday

X is for expert

W is for water

V is for variety

 I is for I the active learner

 J is for joining

 K is for knowing

 L is for looking & listening

 M is for mixing

First-hand experience:
what matters to children

An alphabet of learning from the re

Diane Rich
Mary Jane Drummond
Cathy Myer
with **Annabelle Dixon**

 exploring the world

  U is for under my feet

 T is for thinking

 S is for surfaces

  R is for rain

 **Q** is for questions

  P is for pattern

   O is for out & about

  N is for night sky & night time

 thinking about the world

We dedicate this book to our dear friend and colleague
Annabelle Dixon
(1940–2005)

in memory of her work with children and adult educators.

A donation from the sale of each book is made annually
to the charity, Save the Children, in memory of Annabelle.

First published in 2005 and reprinted with minor amendments in 2006
Revised edition 2014
Rich Learning Opportunities

ISBN 978-0-9549683-2-8

© 2014 Rich Learning Opportunities
   Diane Rich, Mary Jane Drummond and Cathy Myer

Printed by Kingfisher Press, Bury St Edmunds, Great Britain
Layout and design, authors and designer and illustrator, Dave Cousins
                          email dc.bass@yahoo.co.uk

British Library Cataloguing in Publication Data
A catalogue for this title is available at the British Library

Additional copies are available from
Rich Learning Opportunities
www.richlearningopportunities.co.uk

Contents

Acknowledgements

Materials in this book have been trialled by 66 educators from 18 different settings, in eight LEAs.

The authors are very grateful to all those who gave up their time to come to meetings, and to work in their settings with children, parents, colleagues and governors, to introduce and work with these materials and provide valuable feedback.

The settings represent a mixture of rural, urban and multicultural areas. A variety of educators took part, including headteachers, centre managers, class teachers, support staff, nursery nurses and class room assistants. Those taking part were:

Cheryl Barlow, Ann Blanchard, Frances Chesnick, Ana Clark, Clare Clarke, Sarah Clark, Sian Davies, Sarah Day, Vicky Dean, Charlotte Devereux, Judy Dunne, Margaret Dunlop, Liz Du Toit, Lynne Edwards, Jacqueline Egan, Sue Fenwick, Christine Fulcher, Gemma Fry, Helena Garibaldinos, Jenny Gordon, Belinda Handley, Laura Harrisskitt, Anne Hawkins, Hilary Hollick, Lynne Howell, Bernie Jackson, Helen Laws, Marion Leeper, Jenny Maguire, Judy Major, Eileen Martin, Melanie Mathison, Julie Mellor, Ann Mitchell, Cristina Modestou, Rachel Myer, Lucy Newton, Carol Nind, Suzanne Odhams, Sue Papaspyru, Maria Park, Alison Peacock, Terry Pearson, Wendy Perry, Caroline Price, Sarah Roberson, Ann Robinett, Alison Rowbotham, Tessa Roworth, Sue Shaw, Tricia Shingles, Karen Spring, Sonal Thakore, Carly Tilney, Sharron Tingey-Wess, Claire Toberman, Rachael Tomlin, Ann Warren, Jane Whitehurst, Susan Williams, Helena Worley, Georgina Wray, Rosemary Zelli.

There may be other educators who supported those listed above, whose names we have not been given. We are grateful to them all for their support.

Grateful thanks to Jane Lane for her useful comments on drafts and to Miki and Ian for proof reading.

We also thank John Messenger and John Myer for their support, encouragement and cheerfulness throughout the writing of this book.

The authors thank all the young artists and writers who have allowed us to include their artworks and writing in this book.

We are very grateful to artists Andy Moss and Jamie Wardle for permission to include their work on *The Fallen 9000*.

The What Matters to Children team

The What Matters to Children team was active from 2004-2012.

The group was made up from respected education consultants, authors, researchers and educators. Their work was co-ordinated by Diane Rich, Rich Learning Opportunities.

The What Matters to Children team came together to develop the thinking introduced in the original publication of this book and later the extended ideas in their second publication, *Learning: what matters to children* (2008). They supported educators in developing what matters to children by designing and delivering many day and residential conferences, training sessions, work in schools in England and beyond, and at the Science Learning Centre for the East of England, and its national centre in York.

Several members have now retired, but many continue to work actively in different areas of education. The group included

Denise Casanova	Emma Hertzberg	Diane Rich
Jacqui Cousins	Jennie Lindon	Simon Small
Annabelle Dixon	Cathy Myer	Janet Snook
Andrea Durrant	Rachel Myer	Jane Turner
Mary Jane Drummond	Marjorie Ouvry	Sue Pearson

The authors of this revised edition are extremely grateful to each and every former team member for everything they have contributed to our thinking over the years, for their dedication, intellectual energy, professional companionship, support and laughter and especially for their parts in forming, firming and living our principles.

Thank you to each one of them.

About the authors

The authors are a team of experienced and respected education consultants. They have come together to work on a variety of projects for many years, and have always been committed to promoting what matters to children. In 2008, Diane Rich, Mary Jane Drummond and Cathy Myer co-wrote *Learning what matters to children*.

Mary Jane Drummond is a writer and researcher with an abiding interest in young children's learning. Before retiring she worked for many years at the Faculty of Education at the University of Cambridge.

Cathy Myer has been a teacher, advisory teacher, university lecturer. and freelance education consultant. Although now retired, she remains passionate about children and their capacity to learn from their experiences of the real world.

Diane Rich has been involved in children's learning for many years, as play worker, teacher, advisory teacher, researcher, consultant, author and trustee for children's charities. She co-ordinated the What Matters to Children team from 2005-2013 and recently worked as a visiting lecturer at the University of Roehampton. She continues to work as a freelance consultant and runs Rich Learning Opportunities: keeping creativity, play and first-hand experience at the heart of children's learning.

Annabelle Dixon (1940-2005) Annabelle's classroom was, in the words of a friend, 'a place of genuine intellectual search'. As psychologist and teacher she was committed to offering first-hand experiences to children as the essential basis for such a search.

A note about terms

Throughout this book we use the term **we** to refer to the authors.

We use the term **educator** to refer to all those who work in a professional capacity with children form birth to 11; carers, childminders, play workers, nursery nurses, teachers, teaching assistants and students. The term **teacher** is used in some learning stories.

We use the term **school** to refer to permanent locations where educators work with children, including maintained schools and independent schools.

We use the term **setting** to refer to any out-of-home location for children from birth to 11.

Learning stories have come from schools and settings from rural, urban and city based areas of both social deprivation and privilege.

Foreword
Pain, love, loss, looking and learning

by Tim Smit

There is a famous doggerel Confucian saying which holds that 'wise men do not learn from experience, but from the experience of others'. It sounds good, but like so much marketing speak it is only a partial truth. For instance, you don't need to bang your head on a brick wall to know that it hurts, but the same is not true of the generic need to experience pain; only by going through it do you know how much you can take and what you might be able to put up with in survival situations. The same is true of almost any fear; confronting it is often the only way to deal with it and to grow as an individual. Many people suffer agonies of insecurity in later life because they have avoided anything unpleasant. The fear of fear creates in them a paralysis that inhibits their dealings with people and situations; this ultimately leads to a greater unhappiness than if they had dealt with pain head on, for themselves.

I start from a serious premise in order to put experience into context. In any situation, both passive observer and active participant are subject to an experience. The former learns vicariously from the lived experience of the other. The latter experiences it directly, but in being so focused may not see the whole. Each will have learned different things. I am arguing that both kinds of learning from experience are important in building up a palette of responses to a huge range of situations, but the lessons are qualitatively different when they concern cause and effect – the consequences for one's feelings, both physical and emotional. These are exclusive to the participant. To say that it is better to have loved and lost than never to have loved at all can only be said and meant by someone who has loved, for the observed behaviour of the abandoned lover would appear to contradict it!

My childhood was rich in smells, noises, warmth and little frissons of terror – mostly of my own making. I climbed trees with daring, but was hugely frightened. I lifted stones wherever I went in order to inhale the smell of moist earth and the slightly lemony hay smell of crushed bracken.

My thrills were slow worms and toads. There was pond dipping and racing water boatmen, catching sticklebacks and grazing my knees falling off bicycles and out of trees. I spent hours banging random chords on pianos and imagining the worlds to which they formed the soundtrack. Often I took my shoes off and loved the tickly feeling of cut grass, the swishy feeling of long grass, the irresistible roughness of hard sand, and the exotic caress of dry sand; but most of all there was mud. How glorious to let it squidge through your toes! And peeling it off when it dried was another sensation altogether.

David Byrne, of the American group Talking Heads, once wrote a profound song called, I think, *'The Naming of Things'*. It describes a young child in a garden listening happily to the birdsong. When his mother sits down and names each bird, the child can hear it no more, until eventually the garden is silent to him. This is a profoundly melancholy notion; I suppose it matches the cautionary tale about the man who knows the price of everything, but the value of nothing. It's funny though, that as I have got older, I realise that I have to work harder at enjoying simple pleasures, because I have become selfconscious of them.

The most important single event in my sensory life was when a good friend asked me to give him one hour of my time to do exactly as he demanded. I trusted him and agreed. He took me to a field and marked out a metre square of grass. He made me sit and asked me to stare at it for a full hour, maintaining my concentration. To start with I saw grass. Then I saw a spider, then an ant, more ants, more spiders, beetles, a shrew, and within the hour my world had turned upside down. I had looked through the keyhole at a micro-world heaving with life, all of it oblivious of me. How was it possible that I had been so unaware of this complexity? Don't get me wrong, I knew a fair bit about ecology, but knowing it as a theory, and really being aware of it and feeling it, are different.

From that moment on I have been an angry man. My target is all those sloppy people who casually use phrases such as 'the world is so much busier and faster today'. I rant at them and I sneer. How many paces is it from your front door to the gate? How many lamp posts are there on your street? What colour is the light? I take my young Eden Project team members down to the pub on a Friday. 'What are you trying to achieve with the project?' they ask, bright eyed and keen. 'Close your eyes,' I demand. They do as they're asked. 'Please describe the person next to you; colour of eyes, jewellery, hair and so on. Tell me what is on the table. The beer you are drinking: where do the bubbles form – on the side or in the middle? What colour is it? If you must smoke, tell me, how does the smoke curl?' Stunned, most of them fail the test miserably. Strangely, it always appears that the quietest among them seem to have most of the answers now. The mouthy ones are lost. This is a great lesson for any leader; don't confuse quiet or shy with the absence of something to say.

This, I declare, is one of the major things the Eden Project is about. Observation. It is both the foundation of all good science and also the basis for learning from your experience. The world is no faster today than it has ever been. We are merely skating quickly over the top rather than dealing with it or understanding what it is.
'Older and wiser'. There's a phrase. With age you just get older unless you observe closely and allow yourself to feel. Travel broadens the mind – or, does it? To tick off the Pyramids and the Taj Mahal is nothing

if you can't feel anything, sense anything, save the thrill of having seen it. No more significant than answering a question correctly on a quiz show. However there are two common phrases I can recommend, 'waste not, want not'– for here, you are living with the grain of nature. And 'variety is the spice of life' – for here lies enlightenment and the only way of knowing this to be true is to experience it both passively and actively, for yourself.

First-hand experience is perhaps the most important foundation stone in discovering who you really are, and what you might become. Without huge dollops of it, encouraged and nurtured, but rarely directed, we can never become more than the sum of other people' lives, experienced at second-hand. The nightmare vision of a world of non-biologically related clones is an hysterical oversimplification of a possible future. The antidote is to take a few risks, and to let the mud squidge through your toes from time to time. Read this book. It may save lives.

Tim Smit
Chief Executive, The Eden Project
Bodelva
Cornwall
PL24 2SG
www.edenproject.com

The Eden Project. Home of the Eden Trust. Charity No. 1093070

Part One
Introduction to the revised edition

What is this book?

This book is an alphabet of first-hand experiences. The text for each letter has been designed as a springboard from which children, teachers and other educators can launch themselves into the beautiful, mysterious, physical world in which we all live, looking and listening, tasting, touching, and breathing it in.

Why did we write it?

When we sat down to write the first edition of this book, ten years ago, we were well aware that there was no shortage of advice and guidance for educators working with children from three to eight years of age. Our intention in adding to those materials was to support educators in thinking more deeply about one particular aspect of children's learning in those years: their active learning, which is stimulated by high quality first-hand experiences.

At the time, our recent professional experiences of working with early years educators in England had convinced us that many of them had been affected by downward pressures from Key Stage 1 (KS1) and beyond; in KS1 the pressure to achieve high SATS results for six and seven year olds was undeniably affecting the breadth and balance of activities offered to children, with achievements in the core subjects prioritised over active experiences in the foundation subjects.

It was within that context that we had observed, to our dismay, a serious decrease in the opportunities offered to children to experience at first-hand aspects of the real world, from outside the four walls of their educational setting. Inside the setting we had seen copious paper and pencil activities, and sitting down at a table activities; we had seen children looking at images on computer screens, and cutting pictures out of magazines and catalogues, without experiencing the reality for which these images stand. In classrooms for four and five year olds, we had seen a lesson on taste where there was nothing to taste and a lesson on materials where there were no materials.

We had seen a lesson on babies and toddlers without any living babies, and a lesson on pets using images of pets downloaded from the internet. The lesson plans did not include living experiences to support these second-hand activities.

At the same time, a study of children's experiences in reception classes, which one of us had just completed, documented the rarity of authentic first-hand experiences in a small sample of classrooms in England. Using both quantitative and qualitative methods to analyse 25 hours of target-child observations, the researchers concluded that there was an urgent need to reinstate first-hand experience as a core element of every child's entitlement in early education settings. (*Inside the Foundation Stage,* Adams et al. 2004)

Those findings and our own continuing observations caused us much concern. As we discussed our perceptions of the issues, with the experienced educators with whom we worked, we listened sympathetically to their accounts of the constraints that prevented them, as they saw it, from providing authentic first-hand experiences, on a regular basis, across the curriculum, for all children. Educators talked about the pressures to cover all the learning objectives, to provide evidence, in the form of written work, for every objective, to meet targets, to raise literacy and numeracy standards, to work within the guidelines of the national strategies, to prepare for, and survive, Ofsted inspections, and to complete detailed short, medium and long-term planning sheets. Their thoughtful, sometimes rueful, comments encouraged us to continue with the writing of the first edition of this book, convinced that we could offer something of value to educators looking for support and sustenance in order to work in ways that more actively engage children in exploring the world – and everything and everyone in it.

But the most important message we received from those who trialled draft chapters of this book, and generously gave us feedback, was that we were wrong to suggest that this book was only relevant to children aged three to eight. They urged us to consider the whole age range of early years and primary education, and include materials for everyone working with these children. This new edition is an attempt to respond to that challenging but encouraging request.

As we see it, this book stands alongside the statutory documents for the Foundation Stage and Key Stages 1 and 2 in England. These documents are regularly revised, or rewritten, so that educators have come to expect official frameworks to change as a matter of course. However, these documents describe *what* should be taught, not *how*. Teachers and other educators can always manage the curriculum in the way that best serves the learning of all their children. This book can support all educators who seek to provide a curriculum built on real, worthwhile experiences.

The structure of the book
The pages of the second part of this book are of three different kinds:
  • Alphabet pages
  • Learning stories
  • C, I, K, L, Q, T, X, Z: these pages are different, in different ways, as you will find out.

Alphabet pages
These pages use the same format; they are divided into a number of boxes, each containing concise suggestions for exploring the headline topic (for example, *A is for apples, B is for brushes* and so on). The elements that make up each page are the outcomes of our analysis of the problem as we see it, and our considered views on how best to tackle it. These elements include:

  🌿 what matters to children
  🌿 verbs and nouns
  🌿 big ideas
  🌿 questions worth asking
  🌿 books for children and adults

Each of these is described briefly below. The most important of them is our understanding of what matters to children.

What matters to children: four domains of learning

Being in the world   *Acting on the world*

Exploring the world   *Thinking about the world*

What matters to children
Our analysis of what matters to children is at the heart of everything we have written, both in this book, and its sequel *Learning: what matters to children* (2008). We remain convinced that simply providing 'things for children to do' is an inadequate description of what needs to be done to

improve children's opportunities to experience the world at first-hand. Our position is that the things all children do, should be the things that really matter to them not the things that matter to their educators, or to the authors of helpful advice on provision and resources. Our own thinking about what matters to children is described in full on the page for the letter 'I' which we have used to stand for the active learner, the child at the centre of the whole process of education.

'*What matters to children*' is also represented on every page of this alphabet: we have used these ideas as criteria for the suggestions we make for each area of enquiry.

Food and exercise: verbs and nouns

Our thinking about curriculum and children's learning in the primary years has been influenced by a vivid metaphor used by more than one eminent writer on education: food and exercise. In this book we conceptualise curriculum first, in terms of a nourishing diet of first-hand experiences, and secondly, in terms of manifold opportunities for all children to exercise their growing powers to do, to think, to understand and to act on the world in ways of their own invention. Accordingly on each page of this book there are lists of verbs, suggesting the kinds of active exercise that children could and should take in each area of enquiry. These lists are headed, variously; FIND, COLLECT, DISCUSS, OBSERVE, INVESTIGATE, VISIT, MAKE, PLAY and so on. There are also other lists of nouns, words that suggest the actual things, people, plants and animals that children could and should encounter in their enquiries. Many pages also include a list headed *Toolbox,* which suggests the tools that children might use in their investigations into the world. Some of these lists end with a row of dots... This is not because we have run out of ideas; it is to suggest that now it is the reader's turn to add to the possibilities we have suggested.

The dots are a coded message...**OVER • TO • YOU •**

Big ideas: towards conceptual growth

Our metaphor of food and exercise takes us a little further than nouns and verbs. Accordingly, we also include on each page an outline of the conceptual food that we consider each topic to be best suited to provide. These lists of big ideas show how, in studying small and everyday elements of the real world,

children are also learning to think about big ideas, important ideas with a part to play in their full-time project of making sense of the world, how it works and how it can be made a better place for everyone. We see children in the same way as countless other educators: John Dewey (1938) and Susan Isaacs (1930) in the past, more recently Gordon Wells (1987) and Charles Desforges (1992) and, in the field of early childhood education, Vivian Gussin Paley (2004) and Carlina Rinaldi (2006). Like all these writers and researchers (and many more), we see children as capable and hard-working meaning-makers, continuously building up their understanding of the concepts that hold the world together.

Questions worth asking

On each page we offer some suggestions for puzzling and challenging issues that might arise in the course of children's enquiries. We are NOT suggesting that these questions should be presented to children as they stand, OR that children should be required to answer them, every last one. We ARE suggesting that every topic in this book has the potential to throw up paradoxical and enticing topics for discussion, in the form of questions that should not be answered by an internet search, but only by extended discussion, debate and exploration. Children's own questions are often of this kind, and are an especially fruitful starting point for the kind of thinking-out-loud we are advocating here. This topic is taken further on the pages headed Q is for questions.

Books for children

In these boxes we offer suggestions for appropriate books and stories that can be used to deepen and broaden children's enquiries and interests. For all that our principal concern in this book is with the real world, and children's first-hand experiences of that world, we firmly believe that their learning can always be enriched by the world of books: by poetry, myth, fairy-tale, fable, legend, adventure, romance, dreams and domestic drama. These works sometimes express experiences that are difficult to put into words for ourselves. Reading these books, or hearing them read aloud, can deepen and confirm our understanding. The books we have chosen treat with important experiences and feelings, such as fear and courage, anticipation, joy, being different, disappointment and rejection, being found wanting and being labelled, love, hate, good and evil. Stories and poems that reflect these emotions will assure listeners and readers that they are not alone, that their experience is valid and that empathy, comfort and security are powerfully present in the world.

Books for adults, teachers and other educators

In this revised edition we have also included a small number of selected books that we hope will stimulate adults to think more deeply about the curriculum diet that they offer children. Not all of them are by academics or professional educators; we have included novels, poems, biography and autobiography, as well as books written from the child's eye view of the world.

The role of the educator

Our brief description of curriculum in terms of 'food and exercise' leads us to our view of the role of the educator; we see it in terms of three pressing responsibilities – **to provide, to organise and to value**. First, it is the responsibility of all educators to provide the curricular food that will nourish and strengthen children's powers; their second responsibility is to organise children's intellectual and emotional exercise, their enquiries and experiences so that they are actively and emotionally engaged, exploring those aspects of the world that really matter to them, for themselves, with their own hands and eyes and ears and voices, with their own observations, theories, experiments, discoveries and critical questions. And thirdly, through the regular practice of systematic observation, educators learn to value the learning that they see going on before their eyes. Their attentive and respectful observations place them in a powerful position to document worthwhile learning, for the eyes of their colleagues, for parents, and for all interested others. In the process they will be able to articulate the value of that learning, making a serious and convincing case for the quality of what they provide and organise. Educators will be able to use their observations to plan their next steps, taking account of children's growing understanding and expanding horizons, and matching their plans to children's interests and concerns.

An imperfect world

The world that children encounter, inside and outside their settings, is far from perfect: inequity and injustice are deeply embedded within society. It is the additional responsibility of educators to be aware that concepts of equality and inclusion are of paramount importance in their schools, settings and local communities. Of course, this does not imply that every educator is personally responsible for the influences of the wider world on children and their families. But rather, educators have the responsibility to recognise and acknowledge these inequalities and to commit themselves to working to remove all barriers to social justice.

We see this further responsibility in terms of educators recognising and responding to opportunities for children to learn about prejudice, discrimination, and unfairness. Sometimes this means they will need to unlearn unexamined, negative attitudes to difference and diversity. first-hand experiences of prejudice, discrimination and injustice are painful and damaging; but they are not to be denied or ignored. They can be seen as opportunities for educators to challenge the pervading hierarchies of language, skin colour, gender, culture, religion, ethnicity, disability, in which some people are more highly valued than others. Educators who express their critical awareness of these issues, and who are willing to challenge inequity, play an important part in children learning to live by the values of the harmonious and inclusive society that they deserve.

Learning stories

The book does not include detailed suggestions for classroom organisation, for planning, or for ways of managing this approach. There are already many useful texts on these themes; we have chosen instead to emphasise particular kinds of learning, the learning that is stimulated and fostered by the sustained and continuous provision of authentic first-hand experiences. In addition, most of the Alphabet pages are accompanied by detailed *'learning stories'* offered by educators who are committed to promoting first-hand experience with children. On these pages, readers will find educators' accounts of children learning from first-hand experiences: we have called these pages 'learning stories' in recognition of the ground-breaking work of Margaret Carr and her colleagues in New Zealand in assessing and documenting children's learning (Carr 2001). These accounts also illustrate the planning and organisation strategies used by our contributors, who have participated in putting this approach into practice and who have fascinating learning and teaching stories to tell. We hope that teachers and educators will consider reading these 'learning stories' to the children with whom they work, as an illustration of what other children have learned from studying similar themes and topics, and, perhaps, as a way of encouraging children to write their own accounts of their learning.

Focus on learning

The Alphabet pages of this book are about experiences and opportunities that might stimulate many different kinds of worthwhile learning; the activities we suggest are essentially open-ended and it is impossible to define in advance the learning that will take place as children engage with their enquiries. But in the section *How to use this book*, we include comments about the learning that might results from a study of bags and brushes. We see this as our own 'forecast of possibilities within an arena of opportunities', memorable words from Carlina Rinaldi, which we quote again later.

Snappy quotes

Alongside the books for adults we have also included on each alphabet page short, memorable quotations from an eclectic range of thinkers whose work is important to us. We hope our use of quotations will motivate educators to follow up the ideas of those who inspire them – or challenge or provoke. We do not suggest, or even hope that every educator should agree with every one of these quotations: disagreement and debate are sometimes the most fruitful responses to a new idea, just as learning to understand someone else's viewpoint can be an important part of reflective practice.

C, I, K, L, Q, T, X, Z: *these pages are different*

C is for colourful curriculum

On this page we write about 'a colourful curriculum', an idea suggested by Professor Mick Waters. We describe the generous provision, 'the food', needed for such a curriculum and go on to explain the different verbs of learning, by which children move beyond activity to making meaning of the world.

I is for the active learner

On this page we emphasise our view of children as active learners, who do their own thinking, planning, choosing, making, doing and understanding. Here we revisit our analysis of 'what matters to children' and which kinds of learning are most worthwhile.

K is for knowing

On this page we acknowledge the importance of the kinds of knowing emphasised in official curriculum guidance documents, and argue that, in addition, there are other important kinds of knowledge, linked to the kinds of knowing that matter to children: in particular, knowing, how, where, when, who, and why. We offer a description of some of the things that children do want to know, and can know, with the right kind of support. We suggest that children's thirst for learning encompasses knowing who not, as well as who, how not, as well as how, where not as well as where and importantly, why not, as well as why.

L is for listening and looking

On this page we argue that every first-hand activity engaged in by children involves listening and looking of some kind, sometimes many kinds. We outline the characteristics of worthwhile listening and looking, maintaining that children also need plenty of opportunity and encouragement to talk about what they see and hear, and to express their thinking in different ways. This applies to blind and deaf children too, who, like all children, will be listening and looking with all their senses.

Q is for questions

On these pages we discuss the characteristics of questions that genuinely stimulate children's thinking and understanding, and explain our use of a box on every page labelled *Questions worth asking*. We also consider the importance of children's questions and describe the educator's role in encouraging children to voice their powerful questions, some of them difficult ones, about the world. We detail a practical approach to children's questions written by Annabelle Dixon, our former colleague, explaining how children's questions can be used as the starting points for structured enquiries.

T is for thinking

On this page we summarise some of our own thoughts about children's thinking, the important kinds of thinking that are stimulated and fostered by the first-hand experiences we are promoting on the other Alphabet sections.

X is for expert

In chapter K of our second book, *Learning: what matters to children* (2008) we discuss the proposition that children know more than adults think they do. On these pages, we take the argument further, and suggest that children have much to tell us about their learning, that they are, indeed, experts on the subject. To support this proposition, we give a brief account of the great Polish-Jewish champion of children, Janusz Korczak (1878–1942).

Z is for zigzag through the book

This is the final letter of the alphabet and so we take this opportunity to re-emphasise the big ideas about children's learning that run through the whole book, and describe the way in which educators might plan a zigzag route through the alphabet sections. Although the alphabet comes to an end on this page, we hope that educators who read this far will not see their work as suddenly coming to a close. We warmly encourage educators to build on their experiences of using this book, and to continue to act as critically aware, observant, reflective and inventive supporters of children's learning, offering them countless first-hand experiences to feed their insatiable appetite for the world. We also include here the principles that are the basis for our work, and that we hope will stimulate other educators in doing their own thinking.

Encouraging voices, old and new: the theoretical underpinnings of our work

This book has its roots in documents that were once seen as seminal. In particular, as we wrote we kept in mind key passages from the Plowden Report, *Children and their Primary Schools*, published in 1967, which was read by many teachers, for many years, as a distillation of all that was excellent in contemporary primary education. Whether this condition of excellence ever existed in more than a small minority of schools is debatable, but some of the aspects of the 'Plowden School' are, we believe, just as desirable today, as they were nearly half a century ago.
For example:

> A school is not merely a teaching shop; it must transmit values and attitudes...The school sets out deliberately to devise the right environment for children, to allow them to be themselves and to develop in the way and the pace appropriate to them... It lays special stress on individual discovery, on first-hand experience, and opportunities for creative work. It insists that knowledge does not fall into neatly separate compartments and that work and play are not opposite but complementary. (CACE 1967: 187-8)

It is worth noting that this emphasis on discovery and first-hand experiences in an appropriate environment had already appeared in an earlier, equally significant report, the *Hadow Report on Infant and Nursery Schools*, published in 1933. Some memorable passages from this report are especially relevant to the task we set ourselves in this book:

> The curriculum is to be thought of in terms of activity and experience, rather than of knowledge and facts to be stored… What we desire to see is the acceptance of a different set of values from that which has been usual in the past; less weight on the imparting of an ordered body of knowledge and more on the development of the child's innate powers, less reliance on the artificial life of the classroom, more on the experience to be gained out of doors and the opportunities for provides. (Board of Education 1933: 117-23)

More recently, but alas, strangely neglected ever since its publication, the Rumbold Report (DES 1990) powerfully recommended:

> an approach to learning which emphasises first-hand experiences and which views play and talk as powerful mediums for learning.

Even these brief and selective quotations from historical sources are enough, we hope, to demonstrate that this book is, in an important sense, a reminder of some things we used to know about children's learning, and their need for real world experiences, rather than a radical new departure.

We were equally encouraged by many other authors, some of whose words we have used at intervals throughout the book. Robin Hodgkin's work, *Playing and Exploring*, for example, was a welcome source of affirmation for what we are trying to do

> Rather than ask 'what stick or carrot will make children active in certain ways?' or 'what will make them go in this direction rather than that?' we would do well to turn the problem round and to say: children will go in any case, for it is an expression of their being to be purposeful and energetic.
>
> (Hodgkin, 1985)

Inspiration of a different kind came from the English-born poet and philosopher Denise Levertov, reminding us of our original concern, and powerfully describing her visionary solution to the problem.

O Taste and See

The world is
not with us enough,
O taste and see
The subway Bible poster said,
meaning The Lord, meaning
if anything all that lives
to the imagination's tongue,

grief, mercy, language,
tangerine, weather, to
breathe them, bite,
savor, chew, swallow, transform

into our flesh our
deaths, crossing the street, plum, quince,
living in the orchard and being
hungry and plucking
the fruit.

Denise Levertov

We discussed this poem, '*O Taste and See*', at an early meeting of the project team. One of us had recently visited an infant school set in the grounds of an extensive orchard. It was a bright blue September day, and the trees were groaning with fruit; the grass was full of the fallen purple plums and gleaming apples. But the children were indoors, with the windows shut.

We write this book in the belief that children's lives are better spent
> *'in the orchard and being*
> *hungry and plucking*
> *the fruit'.*

How to use this book

We have already explained that we offer this book as a springboard, designed to launch educators and children into authentic exploration and enquiry into the real world. But it is also important to be clear what the book is not about, as well as explaining what we are trying to do. It is not a prescription for a complete curriculum, nor a framework from which to construct such a curriculum. It is not a pre-packaged set of lesson plans. It does not contain lists of learning objectives. It does not advocate that educators should take absolute control of children's lives and learning, or that they should stand back and just wait for learning to happen.

One way of explaining how the book can be used is by turning to the influential work of the early years educators in the region of Emilia Romagna, Italy. Their practices, often now referred to collectively and colloquially as the Reggio approach (after the principal city of the region, Reggio Emilia) have been recognised world-wide as having a great deal to offer other educators. Much of the work in their settings for children from birth to three, and from three to six, is based on what they call 'progettazione', a term which loosely translates as 'projects': cross-curricular investigations of the real world (and familiar territory to early years and primary educators practising before 1988 and the structures of the National Curriculum and the Early Years Foundation Stage, for example). What is distinctive in the Reggio approach to projects is the educators' part in planning them – or rather the absence of planning as we currently think of it. They do not write short, medium or long term plans, in the English way, or work from a pre-defined curriculum of units and sub-units. But neither do they rely on chance or improvisation.

Instead they employ a process that Loris Malaguzzi, the revered champion and pioneer of the approach, calls 'reconnaissance', in which the educators embark on a reconnaissance flight over all the human, environmental, technical and cultural resources. (in an interview printed in Edwards et al. 1993:85)

> Each of the Reggio children's projects begins with a prologue phase, in which information and ideas are shared; predictions and hypotheses are made about what could happen as children bring to the project their different understandings and experiences. So ideas fly, bounce around, accumulate, rise up, fall apart and spread, until one of them takes a decisive hold, flies higher and conquers the whole group. Whatever it turns out to be, the adopted idea in turn adopts the children and the teachers.
> (Malaguzzi, quoted in Fraser and Gestwicki 2002:176)

This is the process that this book is designed to stimulate; it is, in a sense, a companion guide to the reconnaissance or prologue phase of an enquiry, or centre of interest and study. Using this book, teachers and other educators can review some possibilities for the direction their children's enquiries might take. The key word here is possibilities: the ideas we present are only possibilities. We do not intend the suggestions we make to be used in any particular order, or to take up pre-specified periods of time. The issue of coverage has no place here: the issue of compulsion is entirely absent from our proposals. The educators who use our book, will, in consultation and negotiation with their children, make selections from our material and, more importantly, invent imaginative additions and extensions of their own.

Focus on learning: bags and brushes

These two pages explore very similar possibilities, with common themes and conceptual form. The children's task is to search the world for variety and diversity: their discoveries will lead them to understand how this fragment of the world works – as long as they have plenty of time to talk about the big ideas they encounter and to represent them in a variety of ways, in their talk, in their play, in their dance and music making, in their drawings, models and paintings.

The educators' task is to organise and stimulate enquiry, engagement and detailed discussion of the collections that children create (with encouragement and support from you and the children's families), and the observations they make of real things in the real world.

Working with bags and brushes will strengthen children's powers
- to do (notice, observe, record, use tools, collect, search)
- to think (classify, compare, analyse, predict, reason, justify)
- to understand (form and function, diversity, causality, reversibility)
- to represent and express (in talk, in models, in construction, in play, in movement, in music and sound).

As children work with bags and brushes, or any of the first-hand experiences suggested in this book, they will learn what the world is made of and how it works, not just in terms of the things and the materials things are made of - but in terms of ideas. The ideas they will learn about are important ones, with a necessary part to play in the children's full-time project of meaning making. At the same time they will be learning about themselves, and their powers to ask questions, explore ideas, to debate and discuss, to speculate, to imagine new possibilities.

Our intention is that by stimulating educators' awareness of what could be done (during the children's first-hand study of Rain or Variety, Bags and Brushes, for example) we will, as Malaguzzi suggests, set free some original ideas that will 'fly, bounce around, accumulate'. Their guiding principle is that educators will attentively observe which are the ideas that 'warm up' the children: 'the teachers follow the children, not the plans'. Carlina Rinaldi, until recently the Director of Services to Children in Reggio, puts the same idea a different way:

> ...every project is based on the attention of the educators to what the children say and do, as well as what they do not say and do. The adults must allow enough time for the thinking and actions of the children to develop.
> (Rinaldi 1998: 122-3)

We have designed the book to give educators both strength and help in working in these challenging ways; we do not offer plans, recipes or blueprints. Malaguzzi argues that the task of reconnaissance is 'to startle and push us along new roads.' We echo these aspirations.

Some of the possibilities we have suggested will be more engaging for older children, and some for younger ones. Observant and attentive educators will respond to different interests of younger and older children by looking for opportunities to extend an enquiry or re-energise an exploration. They will also observe the moment when the children's curiosity has moved away, to another theme or focus. The educators' observations will ensure that they do not direct or determine children's enquiries, where they could be supporting and encouraging. Observant educators will take their cues from the children. They will be aware that when adults do all the thinking and questioning, on the children's behalf, the children's commitment to the field of study will be diminished, if not extinguished.

To summarise the approach we are presenting in this book, we can do no better than return to Reggio, and the words of Carlina Rinaldi, who describes the work of the project approach in this memorable phrase:

a forecast of possibilities within an arena of opportunities

Why an alphabet?

In preparing this new edition, we often paused to remember our dear friend and colleague Annabelle Dixon (1940-2005) who contributed so much to the original book, even during her final illness. We have enriched the new edition with some additional stories from Annabelle's classroom, sometimes in her own hand, and with some brief extracts from an unpublished text she had written about her experience as *A Froebel Teacher in the 1990s*.

Early in our discussions we remembered a story Annabelle had told us about an alphabet game, and were inspired to use this child's insight as a starting point for our work. He was right: with the help of the alphabet you **can** investigate everything!

E is for everything

The Alphabet Game

When I worked in a mixed-age class of five, six and seven year olds, the children loved playing with a piece of cloth with the letters of the alphabet stitched onto it, each in its own little square space. They would roll the cloth out onto the classroom floor and fetch a box of assorted objects I had collected, mostly from the insides of Christmas crackers. All these objects could be associated with several different letters. One challenge for the children was to place each object in an unexpected position: the challenge for me was to guess why. With glee they would ask me to say why the little red bus, for example, which could have been placed on R or B was now standing in the square marked S. My mind had to tune in to the logic and sharp observation of a young child, but not for the first time I was defeated. 'It's got a 73 on the front and seven starts with S!' Often they played this game in pairs so I was spared going through all the fiendish examples they thought up, but occasionally they were so pleased with what they'd done I was commanded to take a look. Thus it was that one day a child came to me after a very few minutes to announce he'd finished. Would I come and guess what he'd done? To my surprise the spaces on the alphabet cloth were all empty except the square for E, on which he had heaped, precariously balanced, every single object in the collection. He couldn't wait for me to speak, so pleased was he with his idea. 'Look,' he said, opening his arms expansively, 'You see, it's E! **E** is for everything! '

What is a first-hand experience?

Using real things for a real purpose? But that is true of using coloured plastic cubes to develop a concept of number. These things are school equipment. They are real and really useful, but not what we mean in this book.

We mean much more than that.

We mean experiences that introduce children to big ideas and their own power as learners to act on the world, to explore, to think...

We mean...

Handling and using authentic things-

things that people use in the world beyond the 'school' gate. Real clay to work like a potter; seeds to plant that will grow for the real purposes of wondering, seeing, smelling and tasting; cooking for a party; making music for a concert; using wood and tools to make a rabbit hutch or a doll's house...

Visits to and visitors from-

real people, real places – not necessarily a grand visit by coach, but a visit to a wood, the building site of the new estate; visits from a paramedic (complete with ambulance); a new baby; an ancient tortoise; a bee-keeper; an athlete; a chimney sweep...

Being out and about-

in all weathers, day and night, running in the wind, splashing in the rain, looking at the stars, listening to the owls, crunching through frosty leaves, jumping on shadows, building a bonfire, collecting...

An extract from Aldous Huxley's last novel *Island*, first published in 1962.
(Will is our hero, shipwrecked on an undiscovered paradise type island. Mary is a schoolgirl, assigned to help look after him...)

'Believe it or not,' said Will, 'I've never seen a baby being born.'
'Never?' Mary was astonished. 'Not even when you were at school?'
'Not even at school'...
'You never saw anybody dying and you never saw anybody having a baby. How did you get to know things?'
'In the school I went to,' he said, 'we never got to know things, we only got to know words.'

These experiences are real life experiences.

Without them children have little to draw upon in their talk and play, in their painting and drawing, in their modelling or in their story making, in their growing understanding of the world.

They won't know at first hand the real sensations of acrid, scented, soft, soaking, bright, starlight, quiet, heavy, safe, gentle, noisy, strong, dark, enormous, tiny, cold, wet, delicious, crisp, sharp, rushing, breathless .....

BOOKS for children

Frog	Susan Cooper
Swallows and Amazons	Arthur Ransome
The Curious Incident of the Dog in the Night-time	Mark Haddon
The Storm	Kathy Henderson

BOOKS for adults

The Idiot Teacher	Gerald Holmes
The Wild Places	Robert MacFarlane
Roxaboxen	Alice McLerran
Teaching STEM in the early years	Susan Mooman

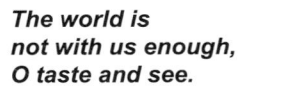

The world is not with us enough, O taste and see.

Denise Levertov

being in the world

 A is for
alphabets & apples

 B is for
bags & brushes

 C is for
collections & colourful curriculum

 D is for
doors

 E is for
enemies

 F is for
furniture

 G is for
goats, goldfish, guinea pigs & other gorgeous animals

 H is for
homes

acting on the world

is for **zigzag through the book** **Z**

is for **yesterday** **Y**

is for **expert** **X**

is for **water**   **W**

is for **variety** **V**

Part two

An alphabet of learning from the real world

 I is for
I the active learner

 J is for
joining

 K is for
knowing

 L is for
looking & listening

 M is for
mixing

exploring the world

 U is for
under my feet

 T is for
thinking

 S is for
surfaces

 **R** is for
rain

 Q is for
questions

 P is for
pattern

 O is for
out & about

 N is for
night sky & night time

thinking about the world

 A is for *alphabets*

WHAT MATTERS TO CHILDREN *a sense of big belonging, knowing the world*

Big ideas: communication representation

This book is an alphabet of real experiences. Each letter can provide a springboard for children to leap into, across and through the world.

Alphabets are systems to make language visible and recorded.
They look different depending on where you are in the world, and when.

China   Europe   Greece
India   Middle Earth   Middle East
Russia   Ancient Egypt

THE PEEP ALPHABET
(invented by Rosie Roberts)

In this alphabet, each letter stands for something that children would use in their schematic play - the play in which children express their pressing cognitive concerns and passionate interests - in, for example,

- *up and down*
- *round and round*
- *connecting*
- *transporting*
- *enclosure and enveloping*

A –*ambulance*	O –*orange*
B –*ball*	P –*parcel*
C –*crane*	Q –*queen*
D –*drum*	R –*rain*
E –*envelope*	S –*suitcase, string,*
F –*fire engine*	*sandwich*
G –*gate*	T –*telephone*
H –*helicopter*	U –*umbrella*
I –*insect*	V –*van*
J –*jump*	W –*windmill*
K –*key*	X –*xylophone*
L –*lid*	Y –*yo-yo*
M –*milk in a mug*	Z –*zigzag*
N –*necklace*	

The word **run** *in Saxon means 'whisper' or what is spoken in a low voice. And that means 'mystery', because what is spoken in a low voice is what one doesn't want others to hear. So* runes *means 'mysteries'; letters are mysteries.*

Jorge Luis Borges

INVESTIGATE

codes
a range of alphabets
writing in a mirror
writing backwards
'secret' invisible writing
the eight letter musical alphabet
Makaton
British Sign Language
Braille
dictionaries
address books
telephone directories
Thesaurus
the Rosetta Stone
scripts
calligraphy
indexes

MAKE

an alphabet for summer, a festival, a friend, the sea, the supermarket, of music
a role play area of a library, a bookshop, a scriptorium
an illuminated letter of the alphabet
a story written in two languages
an alphabet of textures to be read with your fingers
a card index

WRITE with

bamboo
pen brush
chalk
charcoal
computer and keyboard pen
finger
gold leaf
ink
iPad
paint
pencil printing
blocks
quill
stylus
stick…

Splendid words

runes   hieroglyphs   font
illuminate   calligraphy   codex   vellum

Questions worth asking

- Why are there different alphabets?
- Why do we use an alphabet?
- Why does A come first?
- Why don't all alphabets have 26 letters?

WRITE ON

bark, canvas, clay, leaves, paper, parchment, screen, scroll, sand, slate, wall...

Use different alphabets to write

your name
a list
a story
a message
a letter
an invitation
instructions
directions
information
a poem
a tune

Books for children

A is for Artist	Ella Doran
An Abstract Alphabet	Paul Cox
An A to Z Treasure Hunt	Alice Melvin
It`s a Book	Lane Smith
M is for Moose	Charles Patcher
Quentin Blake's ABC	Quentin Blake
The New Alphabet of Animals	Christopher Wormwell
Tell Me a Picture	Quentin Blake

Books for adults

Alphabetical: how every letter tells a story	Michael Rosen
Just my type: a book about fonts	Simon Garfield

Links with

First-hand experience: *what matters to children*   Y is for yesterday

Learning: *what matters to children*   L is for libraries of books

is for alphabets: learning stories

Learning the British Sign Language (BSL) Alphabet

When she was only three, Harrie learned simple sign language in her childcare centre, to help her communicate with one of her young friends. She went on regularly using this for greetings and courtesies as part of infant school life.

At the age of 12 Harrie felt motivated to learn more and went to BSL classes, where she was by far the youngest in the group. At 13 she was nominated by her teachers for the 'young learner of the year award' and was shortlisted.

Harrie, now 16, is very competent in BSL. At her swimming club she supports deaf children from four to nine years of age, as well as one entire family, who communicate by signing.

Although many words and some phrases have a single sign, Harrie often uses her BSL alphabet to spell out a word letter by letter, especially when she is chatting informally.

Harrie puts her interest down to her early interactions with children who had difficulty in communicating. She recalls in particular three friends: one with Downs syndrome, another who was autistic, and another who was profoundly deaf.

Harrie has ambitions to go to university and eventually support children with communication difficulties, using sport to break down barriers.

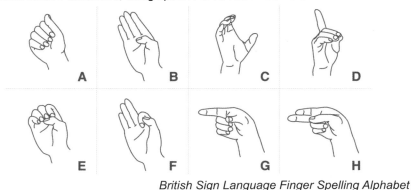

British Sign Language Finger Spelling Alphabet

Local calligrapher

In the autumn of 2013 Barry Jones, a calligrapher living in a small rural village, visited the British Library to see the oldest intact European book: a tiny copy of the Gospel according to St John, believed to have been written by monks at Jarrow Abbey in the late seventh century and given to St Cuthbert of Lindisfarne. The book is known as the *St Cuthbert Gospel.* Barry Jones was so amazed and inspired by this tiny, exquisite book that he made a copy of the opening verses which he presented to his local church.

His work generated great enthusiasm among the village residents who asked him to teach them calligraphy. The subsequent workshop in the village hall was attended by residents aged seven to 70 years. They learned how to attach a nib to the dipping pen, to slide on a reservoir, to load the nib with ink and to make their first attempts at the uncial script used in the original book. This script has no capital letters and is only four nib-widths in height, presenting a challenge for those who were only just mastering the rudiments of writing at school.

Having learned something of this skill the children met again a few weeks later to design Christmas cards. The originals were sold in aid of a children's charity but some were copied and given to village residents, and of course, to Barry Jones.

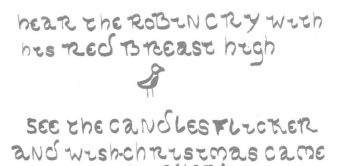

Calligraphy by Hannah, age 12

 A is for apple

Big ideas: inner and outer, parts and wholes, classification, naming, growth, transformation

Plan, plant and tend a flower bed for bees

MAKE

RECREATE a still life of apples painted by, for example, Cezanne
William Morris was inspired by nature.
DESIGN a print inspired by apples.

This is the first apple I have ever picked from a tree. I am so excited. This is wonderful. They do not grow in my country.
Jon, age 39, from Iceland

I have a picture in my head: me with my mum and dad at the table. Dad peeling an apple. He uses his pocket knife and completes the process in one continuous spiralling curl of green. (It's always a green apple.) That's the challenge, of course, to remove the peel, all of it, unbroken. Then we eat the apple. Then we eat the peel. Two different tastes and textures for the price of one, distinguished and revealed by my clever dad.
Allan Ahlberg (2013)

Toolbox

a grater, a fruit knife, a peeler
a juicer, a vegetable mill, a corer
a jelly bag

VISIT

an orchard in May and September
a fruit farm
a market
a greengrocer
Adopt an apple tree and visit it once a month; draw it, photograph it, observe and discuss the way it changes.

COOK

apples blackberry and apple pie
baked apples   toffee apples   apple chutney
apple jelly
ask parents for their recipes

PLANT an apple seed   **PLANT** an apple tree

COLLECT

apples in art paintings, stained glass, sculpture, prints, photographs…

apple names Worcester Pearmaine, Cox, Russet, Ein Shemer *(from Thailand)*, Benonni *(from India)*
places in the world where apples grow
real apples and place them in a colour line
real apples and place them in a size line
(from crab apple to Bramley)

apple part words
peel, skin, stalk, core, ½, ¼, ⅛ pip, leaf, flesh, windfalls...

apple products search the supermarket shelves

apples in a variety of languages

taste apples every possible variety

Curiosities

custard apple, fir apple, crab apple, the Big Apple, Adam's apple, the apple of my eye~ whatever do they mean?

INVESTIGATE

how to change apples – cooking, juicing, pressing, straining, baking...
the connection between the Roman goddess Pomona and a pentagram
how apple trees grow…
espalier, cordon, fan...
the apples of Kazakhstan...
the smallest apple   the biggest apple   the reddest apple...

PLAY

Play or dramatise stories with apples in them, such as

Snow White

The Giants' Feast

Mr Peabody's Apples

play apple games
bob apple,
apples on a string

Questions worth asking

- What is the difference between an apple and a tomato?
- Is an apple dead or alive?

Books for children

Adam and Eve and the Garden of Eden Jane Ray
Johnny Appleseed Reeve Lindbergh
Mr Peabody's Apples Madonna
Orange Pear Apple Bear Emily Gravett
Secrets of the Apple Tree Carol Brown
and Alyssa Nassher
Snow White Jane Ray

Poems

Moonlit Apples John Drinkwater

Books for adults

The Apple Book Rosie Saunders
Liberty Hyde Bailey: essential agrarian and environmental writings Zachary Michael Jack

Links with

First-hand experience:
what matters to children

V is for variety

Learning:
what matters to children

T is for learners
take time

A **is for** *apple:* ***a learning story***

Visiting an orchard

The children in this story are aged four to six years in a small rural school. Just after the summer holidays one of the children, whose mother worked at the local orchard, came to school with a basket of apples. The children wrote to thank her, and at their teacher's suggestion, asked if they could come to visit the orchard.

The following week, armed with clipboards, paper and grade B pencils they walked up to the orchard. The trees were laden with fruit, at child-height, and the children were intrigued by the different varieties, each with its own name. They picked apples and ate them to see which kind of apple they preferred. The bright red ones were declared the best. The children then spent the afternoon drawing the trees, individual trees and rows of trees, drawing the beehives, learning about bees and pollination, drinking the apple juice made at the orchard and buying sufficient fruit to make apple pies back at school.

The following days were apple days. The pies were made, enough for school dinners, and apple jelly. The children modelled apple shaped pots from clay. These were fired, glazed and filled with the delicious jelly. The children learned about their locality and the contribution the orchard makes to the community; they learned that apples come from trees; that you can't have apples without bees – what a startling, unexpected fact. They learned that there are many different kinds of apple and that apples can be used in different ways: to eat raw, to cook, to make juice and jelly. They learned to look and record their observations in drawing and clay; they measured, chopped, mixed, baked and strained juice through a jelly bag; and they learned about buying and selling. They know that apples don't originate in plastic bags, weighed and packaged for the wholesaler. These children have been 'living in the orchard'.

Drawn by four and five year olds at Thongsley Fields Primary School

 B is for bags

WHAT MATTERS TO CHILDREN *finding out what the world is made of, making collections*

Big ideas:
- variety
- diversity
- scale
- fitness for purpose
- transporting
- form and function
- inside and outside

VISIT
Royal Mail sorting office
a sleeping bag factory
a handbag shop
a leather workshop
a recycling centre
a bank
a bicycle shop

Visitors
a bagpipe player

Questions worth asking

- What makes a bag a bag?
- Is a sack a bag?
- Is a suitcase a bag? What about an envelope? A scabbard?...
- What is the difference between a basket and a bag?
- Are some bags baskets? Or some baskets bags?
- What can't you put in a bag?

FIND OUT
Why are there so many plastic bags
What happens to them when they've been used?
Look at the printing on bags- words and pictures- what is it for?

SEARCH for bags....
indoors and out
the smallest bag
the largest bag
find the right bag for the job

> A fishing net is a good bag for carrying fish, but not so good for carrying water!

COMPARE bags
Which bag would be best for what?
Discuss how to find the best bag for the job

GROW
tomatoes in a bag

PLAY
provide a variety of bags for play
organise opportunities to play bag stories
document the narratives of play

...fantasy play is the glue that binds together all other pursuits, including the early teaching of reading and writing skills...
Vivian Gussin Paley

Links with
First-hand experience: *what matters to children*
C is for collections
Learning: *what matters to children*
I is for learners imagine

Precious bags
a doctor's bag
a princess's bag
moneybags
a bag for carrying a crash helmet

COOK edible bags
samosas
ravioli
Cornish pasties
empanadas
dolmades

MAKE
rowanberry jelly using a jellybag
a shopping bag for a mouse or gnome
a sleeping bag for a teddy
a bag for an umbrella
a bag to put a wet dog in
a handbag for a witch and fill it with her possessions
an exhibition of the most interesting bags

We hold that children's understanding is better fostered by meeting their natural interests in the world as a whole, and using their spontaneous impulses to handle and explore, than by giving set lessons in history, geography and the 3 R's.
Susan Isaacs

CLASSIFY bags...
by function - satchel, rucksack, sleeping bag, tea-bag, saddlebag
by owner -   postman, doctor, hiker, cricketer
by fastening - button, zip, string, velcro

Books for children

Crocodile, Crocodile	Peter Nickl
Don't Forget the Bacon	Pat Hutchins
Handa's Surprise	Eileen Browne
My Granny's Purse	Paul Hanson
The Lighthouse Keeper's Lunch	Ronda and David Armitage
The Mitten	Jan Brett
The Paper Bag Princess	Robert N. Munsch
The Adventures of Odysseus	Hugh Lipton and Daniel Morgan

Books for adults

A Time of Gifts	Patrick Leigh Fermor

is for brushes

WHAT MATTERS TO CHILDREN *making sense of the world, understanding how the world works*

Big ideas: causality
fitness for purpose
dentity and difference
transformation and reversibility
classification

The clean dishes don't stay clean

Let's put all the ones with handles together

Van Gogh must have used a very fat brush for this bit

I wonder how many different hairbrushes there are…

You can't sweep a yard with a toothbrush

provide a mystery brush - speculate

LIST
the functions of
brushes
cleaning
applying
polishing
smoothing
adding
covering
playing the drums…

VISIT
a car wash
a train wash
a riding stable
an artist's studio
the caretaker's cupboard
a cabinet maker
a jazz band
a curling team
a chimney sweep at work
and more…

Visitors
a calligrapher   a sign-writer   a water-colourist
a drummer with drum-kit

Watch (children's) interest… listen to their questions… Then you will not be able to doubt the strength and spontaneity of their wish to know and understand.
Susan Isaacs

MAKE
a mascara brush for a giant

a carwash for
James Bond's cars

a nailbrush for an elephant

a hairbrush for a lion

Links with
First-hand experience: what matters to children
V is for variety

Learning: what matters to children
J is for learners do joined up learning

COLLECT *(and organise your collection)*

look in the kitchen
bottlebrush, scrubbing
brush, dustpan and
brush, vacuum cleaner,
pastry brush

don't forget to ask children's parents - they will want to contribute

look out of doors
besom, cow's tail, grooming horses and dogs,
street cleaners, carwash, a fox's tail, ostrich
feathers

look in the bedroom and bathroom
nailbrush, toothbrush, mascara, hairbrush, nail
varnish brush

look in stories
broomsticks!

USE all these brushes

Questions worth asking

🍃 What's the difference between a brush and a comb?
🍃 Is a teasel a brush? Or a hedgehog?
   Or a doormat?
🍃 If you haven't got a brush, what can you use?
🍃 Are there some things that CAN'T be brushed?
🍃 If you were a Borrower, what brushes would you borrow and
   what would you use them for?   (Arietty's hairbrush was made
                       from a human bean's (being's) toothbrush.)
🍃 What makes a brush a brush?
🍃 Why are there so many different brushes?
                       (see also questions worth asking about bags)

Music

LISTEN TO drummers using brushes.
PLAY the drums with brushes

Books for children

Hair   Gerald Rose
Meg and Mog   Helen Nicholl
                           and Jan Pienkowski
Room on the Broom   Julia Donaldson
The Borrowers   Mary Norton

Books for adults

I Learn from Children   Caroline Pratt

C is for collections

WHAT MATTERS TO CHILDREN *knowing the world, making a world map*

Big ideas:
sorting and classifying
inclusion and exclusion
order and pattern

THINK ABOUT
separate   unique
alone   individual
isolated   single
distinct
sole

several   many
together   cluster
group   set

LOOK AT *a painting of a collection*
My Gems   William Harnett
Letter Rack   John Peto
MAKE a painting or drawing of
your own collection

Patterns are made with collections
- **natural objects** look at the environmental sculptures of Andy Goldsworthy and Richard Long
- **made objects** buttons, pom-poms, keys, wing nuts, screws…
- **printmaking tools**
- **mark-making tools** look at the painting 'Lines of Marks' by Wassily Kandinsky
- **numbers, sounds, dance sequences**

VISIT
a concert what is on the programme? Is the music a collection by one composer or by several? Is there a choir?

an art gallery find a collection of paintings about a theme such as stories, big events, food, special people, journeys. Paint your own picture to fit with the collection.

a museum what collections have been made by other people – fans, armour, trains? How can you arrange your own collection?

a nursery choose a collection of plants and explain why they go together

a library borrow a collection of books about... castles, frogs, giants, pirates, owls... or by the same author.
Borrow music sung by the same artist, written by the same composer, played on the same instruments, or other ways to make a music collection.

Collections of people
crowd, party, class, school, congregation, choir, nation, parliament, demonstration, march, group, society, club, friends…

Collective nouns
army, band, brood, flight, cluster, clutch, flock, gaggle, herd, team, litter, orchestra, quartet, shoal, swarm

Links with
First-hand experience: *what matters to children*
P is for pattern
Learning: *what matters to children*
C is for learners choose

badges, books, buttons, cards, erasers, feathers, gemstones, hats, pebbles, pencils, postcards, ribbons, rubber bands, shells, stamps, superheroes... what is missing?

Questions worth asking
- What makes a collection?
- How many make a collection?
- Is everything part of a collection?
- Is there anything that does not belong to a collection?
- What is the opposite of a collection?
- How many people make a crowd?
- How many is many?

MAKE collections of words
wet words   dark words   small words
blue words – navy, turquoise, sky, royal, Delft
guinea pig words

MAKE *a collection of patterns*
Rangoli, Kente, Adinkra, Mehndi, Paisley, Morris and Co. wallpapers, wrapping papers...

MAKE A LIST OF
shopping for a picnic
things to do
holiday packing
names for my baby
places to visit by bus
favourite stories
friends for a party

Books of collections
alphabets
dictionaries
photograph albums
thesauruses
counting books
phone books
crossword puzzles
recipes
postcards
short stories
poetry anthologies
song books
make your own

Children are full time researchers, untiring remakers of actions, ideas and theories.

Loris Malaguzzi

Books for children
Frederick   Leo Lionni
Frog and Toad Make a List   Arnold Lobel
The Guinness World Records
Guinness World Records
The Willow Pattern Story   Alan Drummond

Poems
The Cat and the Fiddle   Jackie Morris
Overheard on a Saltmarsh   Harold Munro

Books for adults
The Girl with the Brown Crayon
Vivian Gussin Paley
The Hare With Amber Eyes   Edmund de Waal

is for collections: a learning story

Collecting for a photogram

In a small urban Infant school a group of children aged four to seven years watched a DVD of the artist Andy Goldsworthy working with natural materials. They discussed his work and studied the photographs he had made of his sculptures. The children were invited to explore a wild area of the school field and to collect material for their own work of art. For some children this was the first time they had come face to face with daisies, buttercups, tansy and mallow; they realised that grasses also produce flowers. There was time to choose; there was no rush. There were clear guidelines: if there were only a few plants of a particular variety, then pick none; if there were several then pick a few; if there were many, then pick several. Excellent discussion questions: exactly how many is 'a few', 'several' or 'many'? Back in the classroom the children made photograms, arranging their collections on photographic, light sensitive paper. The paper was affected immediately by the sunlight, darkening the space around the collections. The leaves, petals and grasses blocked the light, creating white silhouettes on the paper. The children had to work swiftly because the paper continued to change colour while they worked. The photograms were left in the sun, closely observed by each artist, until the paper was deemed not to change any more. To prevent further change each sheet was placed in photographic fixer, rinsed and left to dry. It would have been quicker to use a camera but this process was new and magical.

The bond with the artist was made. He collected, they collected; he arranged, they arranged; he photographed, they recorded with photograms.

Educators enjoying a similar experience at a conference workshop reflected on their learning. What big ideas had they encountered as they worked? What would their children have learned offered the same opportunity?

The educators wrote the following list of learning:
The power of light and its absence, dark, size, shape, texture, pattern, change, image, silhouette, unique, criteria, procedure, design, respect, beauty, awe and wonder, permanence and impermanence, prediction, chemical reaction, projection, protection, shadow, time, mystery, sequence, exploration, discovery, independence, strategic thinking, the value of sharing.
It is quite a collection.

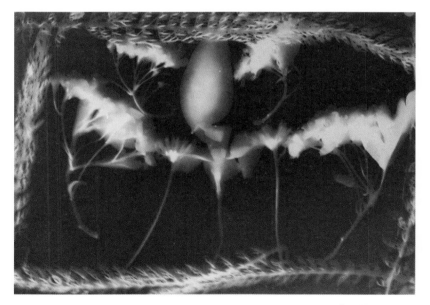

Sophie age six

 **is for** colourful curriculum

WHAT MATTERS TO CHILDREN *making a mark on the world, making my own world map*

Big ideas:

Colour as decoration
variety beauty
change...

Colour as identity
diversity team clan
prejudice justice
compassion
ethnicity...

Colours with function
communication
symbol
sign...

And I believe that children should have a magical curriculum. It should be a curriculum of colour, it should be a curriculum of pattern, it should be a curriculum of delight.

Mick Waters

Questions worth asking

Can you smell, taste, hear, feel colour?

COLLECT AND RECORD
the colours of water
the colours of the earth
the colours of decay

Intriguing words
technicolour
sepia
vibrant
iridescent
translucent
opaque
tint
illuminate
mottled
hue...

PLANT a vegetable garden or a window box

MAKE a mosaic with clay tesserae

BATIK the colours of the sea

PLAY the story of *The Great Blueness*
by Arnold Lobel

WATCH a sunset and a sunrise

DANCE a painting

PHOTOGRAPH a tree every week for a year

Colour in art: COMPARE the works of
Anish Kapoor
Bridget Riley
Georgia O'Keefe
Henri Matisse
J.M.W. Turner
Paul Klee
Wassily Kandinsky
Illuminated manuscripts

VISIT
tropical aquarium
fruit market
jeweller
stained glass windows
theatre

INVESTIGATE
prisms
spectrum
kaleidoscopes
vegetable dyes
camouflage, especially zebras
mixing colours – paint, light, acetates,
papers, pastels, inks...

Music

PAINT to music of different genres: jazz,
pop, reggae, classical, funk, rock,
ballet, Bollywood

ILLUSTRATE your favourite song

LISTEN TO Rhapsody in Blue George Gershwin
Purple Haze Jimi Hendrix

COMPOSE red, green, blue music

Books for children

Chidi Only Likes Blue — Ifeoma Onyefulu
Kandinsky — Michael Robinson
Tar Beach — Faith Ringgold
*The Blue Rider: the yellow cow
sees the world in blue* — Adventures in Art
The Indian Paintbrush — Tomie dePaola

Poems

The Blue and Green Ark — Brian Patten
How to Make a Portrait of a Bird — Jacques Prévert

Books for adults

Rapunzel's Supermarket — Ursula Kolbe
Park Guell: Gaudi's Utopia — Josep M. Carandell
and Pere Vivas Ortis

Links with
First-hand experience: what matters to children
V is for variety
Learning:
what matters to children
see the following Colourful Curriculum learning story

C is for colourful curriculum: a learning story with a difference

This section is one of several that are different throughout the book; it is a learning story with a difference, to illustrate the range and depth of learning that is possible with a curriculum that is active, engaging and full of variety- a colourful curriculum.

What is a 'colourful curriculum'?

The curriculum is what children 'do'; to be worthwhile what they do will be rich in variety, deep with layers of understanding, vibrant, unhurried and joyous. We know children are active learners; we know they like to make, investigate, collect and engage with a rich variety of experiences, those we have described as 'food' in the introduction. But, 'what children do' is more than mere activity, busyness. By acting on the world they learn to belong; to make good choices; to recognise and respond to feelings, their own and those of others; to imagine and to represent their learning.

These are some of the big verbs of learning we describe as 'exercise'.

How does a colourful curriculum give plentiful opportunity for such exercise?

First it will require generous provision: visits to art galleries, to buildings with stained glass windows, to tropical aquaria, fruit and vegetable markets, a theatre projection room to experience the effects of colour change on theatrical sets. It will require visits from a jeweller with a collection of gemstones, a quilter, an embroiderer, a painter. Further provision will include a variety of paints, pencils, pastels, papers, dyes, acetates, fabrics, threads, cameras, IT tools and programs, spices, foods – and the knowledge and capacity to use them.

This is marvellous food.

And what will the learners do with all this?

The following paragraphs highlight ways in which children willl experience the verbs of learning within a colourful curriculum.

Each verb is accompanied by the big ideas children are likely to encounter.

B is for **learners belong to a community of learners**

Big ideas: identity, nationality, inclusion/exclusion

RESEARCH team colours, uniforms, clan tartans, national flags at international events;

USE colour to create a sense of belonging to a team, group, choir or band

---

C is for **learners choose**

Big ideas: characteristics; criteria; variety

FIND and collect the colours of water, earth, decay, trees, sky, beach, vegetable market…

How can these be represented using materials such as paint, papers, fabric, threads, clay?

F is for **learners feel**

Big ideas: expression, empathy

RESEARCH ceremonial colours: parades (Orange Men; Black and Tan); Trooping the Colour; festival of Holi; traditional wedding colours; colours of mourning; colours to depict feeling

---

I is for **learners imagine**

Big ideas: communication; empathy

LOOK AT paintings: Guernica, Picasso; The Last of England, Ford Maddox Brown

PLAY the story of a painting

PAINT a story of your choice

J is for **learners do joined up learning**

Big ideas: connection

VISIT a place rich in colour and then...

MAKE a collection of your favourite colours from it and then...

MIX paint, collect papers or threads, use pastels to...

MATCH those colours and then...

FIND an artist who has also used those colours and then...

RESEARCH artists who painted like this and then...

COMPOSE music to express these colours and then...

DESIGN a room using these colours and then…

 **is for colourful curriculum**

K is for learners know

Big ideas: enquiry, research, hypothesis

GENERATE questions arising from an interest in colour, such as

• what happens to colour in the dark? is red still red?
• who were the Scottish Colourists?
• what was the Blue Rider art movement?
• how was colour a symbol of conflict in the Wars of the Roses?

R is for learners represent their learning

Big ideas: representation, interpretation, translation

PAINT joy, anger, energy (reference the Expressionist movement 1905-1933)

DRAW your favourite place

DESIGN a stained glass window for a local building

BUILD a model stage set with lighting

U is for learners thirst for understanding

Big ideas: investigation, connection, enquiry

EXTRACT dyes from plants

INVESTIGATE prisms, rainbows, spectrums, acetates, light box, light sensitive papers

EXPLORE ways to mix colours with paint, pastels, crayons, ipad

M is for learners make meaning

Big ideas: communication, protection, status

RESEARCH colours used to inform, warn, protect (red warning lights on tall buildings, traffic lights, boats, aircraft, railway signals)

RESEARCH warning colours in nature, on clothing; camouflage in nature, on clothing

RESEARCH colour to depict status: (black mourning bands, white stick for the blind, blue flag for safe beaches, uniforms)

RESEARCH colour to depict place: maps, ordnance and maps of the world

T is for learners take time

Big ideas: patience, persistence, stillness, tenacity, commitment

PLANT a window box

PAINT a diary of the sky every day for a month

LEARN a poem with colourful imagery such as *How to Paint a Portrait of a Bird* by Jacques Prévert

LISTEN TO music: jazz, blues, classical, pop

X is for learners expect the help and truthfulness of grown ups

DISCUSS questions that arise from racial issues and those relating to identity and affiliation (link with chapter Q is for questions in this book).

Exploring colour provides opportunities in abundance for children to learn in ways that matter to them; being, exploring, thinking and acting. Children will desire to continue to learn, to take time, to make connections and to return again and again.

C is for colourful curriculum

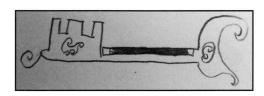

I is for **learners imagine** by Shohan age eight

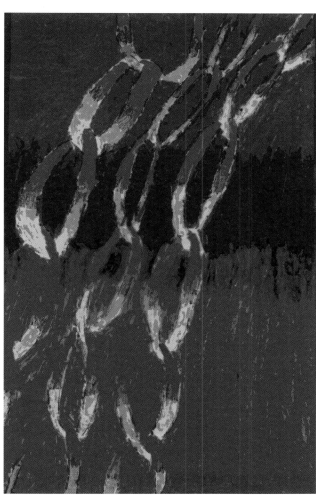

V is for **variety**

O is for **out and about** by Millie age six

 **D** is for *doors*

WHAT MATTERS TO CHILDREN *what is in the world, finding how things work*

Big ideas:
- diversity
- form and function
- fitness for purpose
- human ingenuity
- the familiar is fascinating

EXPLORE

door furniture

hinges

handles

latches

keyholes

eyepieces

bolts

letter boxes

locks…

VERBS

**observe, photograph, draw,
make working models...**

FIND *animal doors*

beehive

mouse hole

whelk

cat flap

stable door

hamster cage

chicken coop

INVESTIGATE

glass doors   sliding doors

revolving doors

lift doors   trap doors

curtains

garage doors   the office safe

zip doors on a tent

fly screens

folding doors   an Advent calendar

secret doors

DISCUSS the function of doors

Keeping things in or keeping things out?

Letting light in or letting light out?

AND…

VISIT

the biggest door – cathedral? guildhall? fire station?

the oldest door

the smallest door

Materials

glass canvas metal

steel plastic rush sea shells

beads mesh

different woods-

oak, pine, cherry, walnut, sapele...

Questions worth asking

- Is a gate a door?
- Is a letter box a door?
- Why don't kennels have doors?
- What makes a door a door?
- Does everything that opens also shut?
- Are there doors that never open?
- Are there doors that never shut?

DISCUSS

Are some doors curtains?

Are some curtains doors?

DISCUSS metaphors

An eyelid is a door to the eye. The lips are a door to…

COLLECT

other things that open and shut

inkwells

umbrellas

suitcases

the sounds of doors

knock knock jokes- make up your own

WRITE AND PERFORM

a symphony of doors

*Every question
is a door handle.*
George MacDonald

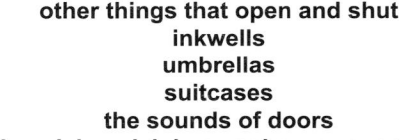

Links with

First-hand experience:
what matters to children

K is for keys

Learning:
what matters to children

E is for learners learn everywhere

Books for children

Doors   Roxie Munro

Sara and the Door   Virginia Jensen

The Rain Door   Russell Hoban

The Sign on Rosie's Door   Maurice Sendak

The Lion, the Witch and the Wardrobe C.S Lewis

Who's at the Door?   Jonathan Allen

Poem

The Door   Miroslav Holub

Books for adults

*Fantastical Guides for the Wildly Curious:
Ways into Hinchingbrooke Country Park*   Deb Wilenski & Caroline Wendling

D is for doors: a learning story

When is a door not a door?

I work with children in a Foundation Stage unit consisting of a nursery, where three and four year old children attend in two groups for half a day each day, and a class of four and five year olds.

Before getting started, I familiarised myself with the major themes of the book. I tried to get to grips with 'what matters to children' as fully as I could. I internalised the 'questions worth asking' for *D is for doors*. I think this really helped me because that way I had the questions ready as prompts, if the right time to use them with children should come up.

I didn't plan anything. I wanted to follow the children's interests and see what happened. It meant a lot of close observing and real listening. In fact, the children didn't spontaneously pursue any investigation of doors. I was disappointed, but going back to the text, I decided to set up a display with 'door furniture' such as locks, handles and hinges. On reflection, there seemed to be more hinges on display than anything. I don't know if this was the reason, but interest in door hinges, and hinges everywhere really took off. I was amazed at the children's responses. Amy commented on the hinges saying,

'You get those on windows and on doors.'

So I asked, 'Can a window be a door?'

Amy hypothesized at great length about windows operating as doors. Beth concluded that

'They both let fresh air in and ladybirds too.'

(We had found a ladybird walking about earlier). She elaborated that we wouldn't need doors if windows came in different sizes for different people and if they could be at different heights. She said that babies needed windows they could roll out of to explore the world, and she mimed top-hinged swinging windows. She obviously saw doors as a problem for babies and their explorations, unlike adults who more often see them as a solution! Her thoughts led to further considerations about how rooms could be built with various different windows for different people.

I drew the group's attention to the hinges on display. Amy again became very interested, focusing on the smallest hinge in the collection, from a jewel box. She said,

'This must have come from a fairy's door. I don't know what has happened to her.'

She held on to the hinge for ages, describing what the fairy looked like and that she lived in the bottom of a tree. The hinge inspired her story and her play.

Carly recognised one hinge in the display as the same type as the one on the door to the toilet. We all went to investigate this, which led to the group wanting to look for hinges all around them. This was not something I had thought of and after sorting out support staff to look after the remaining children, we decided to go on a hinge hunt. We took cameras to see how many hinges we could find and capture the images.

I was really surprised when the children's first stop was in the classroom at the book box. Delia pulled out a book and declared,

'Look! This opens and shuts like a hinge.'

They proceeded to find so many other hinged things - swing bin lids, high level door closers, hinges on easels, window hinges. I was really struck by how much interest they had in hinges. For several consecutive days after, the children brought in hinges or told me of somewhere else they had found them.

The children posed a lot of questions for themselves and were encouraged to explore their own thoughts. For example:

Why does it open this way?

Why do we need doors if windows open?

Not all doors have handles – like on buses.

Are all hinges metal? (Those I'd collected were, but the hinge hunt came up with a different answer.)

The Big Ideas section for *D is for doors*, says 'The familiar is fascinating.' This was certainly so in this case. The experience confirmed for me that the simplest things can be of real interest to children and that many adults who work with and care for children so easily forget this, in our rushed familiar world. We easily forget what it is like to be discovering, perhaps for the first time, something that is right under our noses.

 D is for *doors*

Other things I could have done

I could so easily have let the children run with the idea much further and I am convinced their activities would have covered so many areas of learning.
I tried to scribe the fairy's story, but should have recorded it at the time.

On reflection I realise I needed more practice at this, and to include my teaching assistants too.

I would love to have sent a camera home for the children to have photographed a door to tell us about and will do so next time.

Of course, now it's a lot easier because of digital cameras and, ipods and phone cameras. Practically every family has the means to take photos and email them in.

I regret not arranging for a small delegation of children to investigate bus doors. It would have been possible, at least, for a small supervised group to travel on a bus from one stop to the next one and then take a return journey to report their findings and inspire new questions.

   Do all buses have doors?
   Do any bus doors have handles?

Visits don't have to be grand and involve everyone. A second delegation of different children, or the same ones, could have gone off to investigate even further questions, and report back… then maybe a third?
We could certainly have gone further beyond the school to investigate.

The children's learning

It was quite apparent that the children were engaged in higher levels of thinking. Their genuine interest promoted higher order questioning quite naturally, without me having to plan sessions to cover this. They were more committed, more focused and more interested in what they were doing. All the children kept really busy and stuck at what they were doing. Their interest in door (and other) hinges spanned a range of investigations: gravity, weather, the properties of shapes and the needs of babies. Even their play and story telling were affected by this project.

My learning

This project supports my view that compared to adults, children can have equally interesting, sometimes better ideas, theories and hypotheses about things in the world. They are much more interested in finding the answers to their own lines of enquiry than in any enquiries I suggest to them. I had decided to follow their lead and although at times it was hard to hold back from a direction I wanted them to follow, it was worth it. I really think that the hinge hunt will remain a multi-sensory memory for the group of children involved – they still talk about hinges!

Time passes...

In preparing this revised edition, one of the authors contacted educator, Ann again. She remembered that the Doors project described above, developed into K for keys. She said,
The children DID go further beyond the school gate - we went to Colchester Castle, where we saw some impressive castle doors of all sorts and with a contrast in sizes. The children's fascination for keys started with a mixture of the huge castle door locks and setting up a castle in the class room as a role play scenario. We had real props: floor-standing wrought iron candle holders, real candles, wall sconces and tapestry hangings.
One child brought in keys (ordinary ones) and then more children brought in big metal keys for the castle doors. We collected keys, looked at locks and how they worked, imagined what the keys might open, what might be behind the doors once opened and who might have lost the keys. It involved a lot of play, talk and fantasy, more so than the doors focus, but we still came back to real keys.

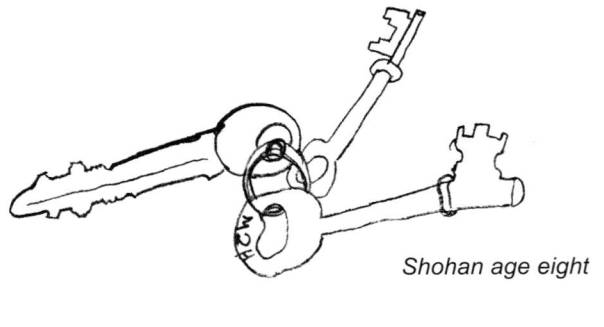

Shohan age eight

And now **K** is for keys appears on the next page of the book.

K is for **keys**

Big ideas: freedom and imprisonment
power and control
protection
security and insecurity

FIND OUT about
Keys as images
in heraldry

unlock a secret

FIND
the oldest key
the smallest key
the shiniest key
the most ornate key
keys for big things
COMPARE ALL THESE KEYS

VISIT
a local street
keyholes in your setting
a church
a locksmith
an ancient building
a state of the art modern building
a second hand furniture shop
the ceremony of keys at
the Tower of London (or similar)

watch a key being cut
(you might need ear plugs!)

INVESTIGATE
What can be unlocked with a key?
What should be locked away? Why?
Which key is the most important key?
Is a password a key?

Questions worth asking
🍃 Is it better to be locked in or locked out?
🍃 Does a key give freedom or
imprisonment?
🍃 What will happen when I unlock
the door…?

INVESTIGATE
skeleton keys   pass keys   house keys
car keys   dimple keys   abloy keys
magnetic keys   four-sided keys
doubled-sided keys   tubular keys
allen keys   keys for meters   barrel keys
key cards…

MAKE a list of everything you can lock and unlock with a key
a diary   a jewellery box
a trunk   a castle door
a safe   a padlock…
and what do you find?

HUNT
for keyholes EVERYWHERE

I kept a five year diary. It had a tiny lock and key…

…keep your own diary

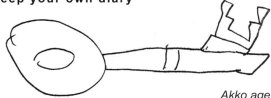

Akko age seven

Key curiosities
Why is Florida Keys so called?   What is a basketball key?
How many musical keys are there? Why are they important?
Where do you find a key on a map?
Who are key personnel?
What keys are there on a keyboard? typewriter? piano?
Which key do you press when asked to 'press any key'?

FIND lost keys

INVENT ways to stop people losing their keys

Books for children
Eight Keys   Suzanne LaFleur
George's Secret Key to the Universe   Lucy and Stephen Hawking
The Keys to the Kingdom (books 1-7)   Garth Nix
Sarah's Key   Tatiana deRosay
Poems
The Key to the Kingdom   Traditional
Books for adults
The Long Walk to Freedom   Nelson Mandela

Links with
First-hand experience: *what matters to children*   **D** is for doors
Learning: *what matters to children*   **I** is for learners imagine

 E is for enemies

WHAT MATTERS TO CHILDREN *with friends, making my own moral map*

Big ideas:
- conflict
- power and control
- love
- friendship

No one is born hating another person because of the color of his skin, or his background, or his religion.
People must learn to hate, and if they can learn to hate, they can be taught to love, for love comes more naturally to the human heart than its opposite.

Nelson Mandela

VISIT
a war memorial
(there are said to be no war memorials in Switzerland. Can this be true?)

Books for children

Best of Friends	Shaun and Sally Anne Lambert
Blade: Enemies	Tim Bowler
Cops and Robbers	Janet and Allan Ahlberg
Dirty Bertie: Pirate	David Roberts and Alan MacDonald
Friend or Foe	Michael Morpurgo
The Iliad and the Odyssey	Marcia Williams
War Horse	Michael Morpurgo
Monster Poems	John Foster and Korky Paul

Books for adults

The Kindness of Children	Vivian Gussin Paley
Boys and Girls: Superheroes in the Doll Corner	Vivian Gussin Paley

INVESTIGATE
Are predators enemies?
Do animals have enemies?
Places where enemies go
Where do enemies come from?
Have I got an enemy?
Am I an enemy?
Can enemies be nice?

MAKE
a place safe from enemies
a place for peace
make a peaceful place

Everyone is your friend until you find out they are not.

George, aged 5

Links with
First-hand experience:
what matters to children

K is for knowing

Learning:
what matters to children

F is for learners feel

Children are the most implacable enemies of boredom

Loris Malaguzzi

Music

Ghillie Callum
    Traditional Scottish sword dance
Jets and Sharks   West Side Story
Purple People Eater   Sheb Wooley
Romeo and Juliet   Sergei Prokoviev
Star Wars   John Williams
The Monster Mash   Bobby Boris Pickett
1812 Overture   Pieter Tchaikovsky

Opposites

love	hate
caring	neglect
safety	danger
friend	foe
conflict	reconciliation
powerful	powerless
leader	member
defend	attack
conquer	liberate
heroes	villains
prejudice	acceptance
destroy	restore

Questions worth asking
- What makes an enemy?
- Do enemies have friends?
- How do you become an enemy?
- Am I an enemy?
- Is it okay to be friends with an enemy?

Let the boys be robbers, then, or tough guys in space. It is the natural, universal and essential play of little boys.

Vivian Gussin Paley

Verbs
loving   hating   caring   fighting
breaking   destroying   crying   dying
rescuing   controlling   befriending
attacking   worrying

Toolbox
role play materials
blocks, planks and blankets for making dens and camps
superhero capes and belts
mini world superheroes

is for enemies: *learning stories*

Where to start?

Many educators reported that although children pursue this theme independently in many different ways, it is rarely expanded and supported as an area of investigation. But when educators looked more closely at the play and questions of children, they saw that children are powerful thinkers when it comes to this theme. The examples below illustrate starting points for encouraging children learning from this area of expertise. Each starting point is from direct observation of children playing.

Thinking about life at home

I work with four and five year old children, and recently a new girl, Sonia, joined my reception class. When she arrived she went straight to the sand tray and played with all the plastic animals, quite violently. And then in the water tray too the animals all fought, under her control.

At the end of the day I talked with her mother. She told me that there were problems at home, lots of arguments and grievances constantly in the air. Routines and stable relationships had been turned upside down. She said they'd been let down by loved ones. The family didn't know who to trust and turn to. It seemed to me that Sonia might have been exploring relationships and conflicts, asking, '*What is an enemy?*' in her play.

Thinking about who are enemies and how to keep safe from them

The same four and five year old children spontaneously played enemies in their small world play and other kinds of play, both indoors and outdoors. They drew pictures of enemies and talked about them as they drew. They listened to stories featuring friends who fall out, such as Pumpkin Soup and re-enacted these in group activities, in role play and using small world story boxes.

This is a sample from a transcript of them at play one day, observed by their teacher.

Orest   Their [enemies'] mummy doesn't teach them to be good. I'm an enemy of someone, but my mummy's teaching me not to be.
Everyone's an enemy of someone. Jack is my enemy, he attacks me…

Kiran   The enemy is attacking your goodie.

Lenny   This one's fighting the tyrannosaurus.

Mike   The T.rex is an enemy because he's got sharp teeth. He's trying to make the enemy dead. The elephant will run away from him…
If you have two enemies they'll be friends. They fight Spiderman.

Orest   He's a baddie, he's got a scary face…

Pablo   If you whack a baddie you might change into a baddie. A baddie might change into an even more baddie.

Quentin   I've made a cage for the dog in case he flies away because he's got wings.

Orest   That's his castle and he's trying to kill my baddie and he can't that's why I put him in my castle.

Ruby   To keep safe from a baddie you can run away.

Shakila I am making a safe place for my cat in a house.

Pablo   He's not an enemy because he's a person... well some enemies aren't persons and some are.

Quentin   …If a goodie hits a baddie then he gets [to be] a baddie.

Orest   Yes, and if a baddie hits a baddie then he gets a worse baddie.

Pablo   T.rex are enemies because they're meat eaters. It was fighting because it wanted to make him dead and eat him.

Orest   You can't eat him because he's got dangerous teeth.

Quentin   Simon's my enemy. But I'm sad because he's not at school today.

The educator said,
'I was amazed that one sheet of paper on enemies could have produced enough work to last me for at least a term. The enemies project …replaced the week when I was going to investigate 'friends', and was infinitely more exciting.'

She noticed that as the children played they reflected on enemies and revealed their thinking about: What an enemy is; what enemies do; how you get to become an enemy; who an enemy is and how you can stop being one; how to be safe from enemies.

Charlie age six

E is for enemies

Children thinking about 'what is a baddie?'

Part of reviewing a play policy, parents in one infant school were asked to watch their children playing at home. One mother became very interested in the play of her six year old son, Vasos. She took notes, even made a transcript of some play episodes, and talked with the class teacher about them. She also gave feedback at a governors meeting and influenced the school policy. Her observations include the following extract:

Vasos was playing with plastic dinosaurs one day

and he said,

Tyrannosaurus is really bad. He is the enemy of all dinosaurs because he eats them. He is a carnivore and can only have other tyrannosaurus for friends. But if he wants to fight the other dinosaurs, he won't be their friend and then he is the enemy of everyone. But that's sad, so maybe he just has one special

T. rex friend...

If you ever saw one (you won't) you couldn't really be its friend. You can't.

(shouting) **YOU CAN'T BE FRIENDS WITH TYRANNOSAURUS!**

I don't think you would be its enemy. And you wouldn't be a baddie. You would just have to hide. The only enemy a T. rex has is another T. rex, if it isn't his friend.

Not you though. It can't be you.

The mother's account of her son's play was the stimulus for the educator to work on themes that were in tune with the questions Vasos was asking in his play.

Children thinking about war

An educator working with four and five year olds, reflected on how work on this theme had begun. She said,

It all started in the run up to last year's Remembrance Day, when I'd heard a reception child ask, '*Why do we have to buy the poppies?*' I was intrigued by the responses from the children.
'*Because there was a war.*'
'*People died and we have to remember them.*'
'*Because there are baddies.*'
'*My Daddy's in the war and he has enemies and one day one of the enemies shot his door down.*'
Then one child asked, '*Do the Germans buy poppies too?*' and our work on enemies could not be halted.

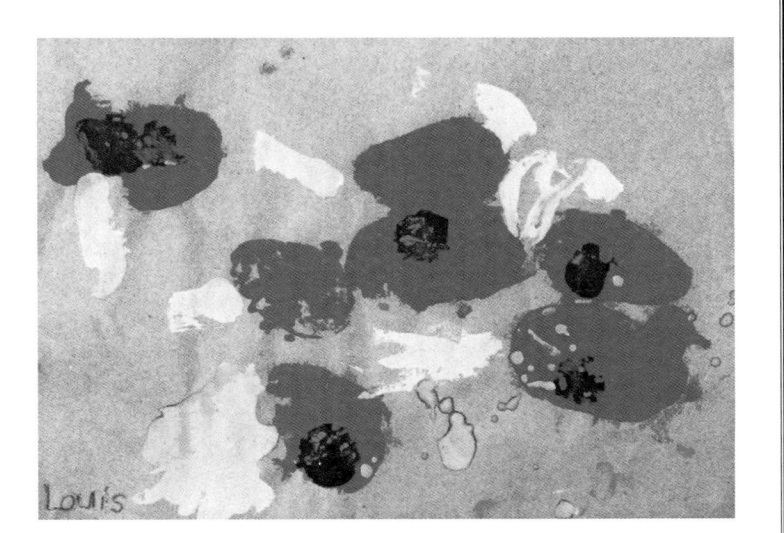

Louis, age three, printed poppies at his nursery when it was the week of Remembrance Day in November.

 **is for enemies**

711,871,176 Reasons Why We Should Remember World War 1

One mother, one father, one wife, two children, two uncles, two aunts and ten friends. Multiply the amount of family members and friends by the 37,466,904 casualties. The answer you get is 711,871,176. This is why we should remember World War 1, not just for the soldiers that died and were injured on both sides, but for the countless families and friends that suffered due to this. Yet this figure is still not reliable, as many soldiers were never found, leaving their families to wallow in grief as the soldier that left them lies motionless in the mud of one of the many battlefields, Ypres, the Somme, Flanders, Verdun, Gallipoli or on of the many other fields of sorrow, unrecognisable, unfound, uncared for by the states of which they bravely threw themselves into battle with outdated tactics. This is why we should remember World War 1.

When one thinks of World War 1, many people will think of the infamous battles such as the Somme or Ypres, almost as if other battles don't exist and when one thinks of the dead, they will think of brave soldiers, proudly wearing their uniforms, charging across the muddy plains against all the odds, and rarely stop to think of the equally brave soldiers who died in the daily exchange of fire between two sides, fighting, maybe not because they believe in any special cause or because they agree with the reasons surrounding World War 1, but because they have to. Irrelevant of who won or lost, each and every soldier who fought on those battlefields, the fields of death, deserves to be remembered due to the sacrifice they and their families paid for a belief of someone they never met. This is why we should remember World War 1. Many lessons can be learnt from World War 1.

For example the widespread use of chemical weapons by both sides in the titanic struggle between the two sides in an attempt to get one over on the enemy, such as that used in Syria by government forces. This caused a horrific casualty rate, especially as in many cases the chemicals would be blown back on their own troops, which does not make the use of chemicals any worse; the mere fact that you're using weapons of this kind is inexcusable. This shows how little the governments of the day thought about their actions, which is another lesson that can be learned, that people must think about their actions before committing to it. This was a painful lesson to learn, especially since the Treaty of Versailles was so harsh on Germany, it led to the rise of Adolf Hitler, another world war and a another sixty million people dying.

Another lesson that can be learnt is that of innocent people suffering as a result of an event that is not their fault. When allied ships blockaded Germany, cutting off a lot of supplies, people starved and generally suffered as a result of the supposedly 'good' side trying to stop supplies getting to the armies of Germany, Austria-Hungary, and Turkey. People suffering as a result of an event that is not their fault can be linked to Syria, with millions of people displaced and around 100,000 people dead. For all the people that died or were injured due to these reasons, this is why we should remember World War 1.

In the words of George Santayana, Spanish philosopher, poet, essayist and novelist,

'Those who cannot remember the past are condemned to repeat it.'
This is why we should remember World War 1.

Louis Thomas-Messenger, age 12

This moving account was written by a 12 year old boy to explain why WWI should not be forgotten.
Louis' convincing and passionate piece won him a prize to visit battlefields of World War I in France and Belgium, including the Somme and Ypres, as well as many war memorials, mainly British, but one French and one German.

 **is for** furniture

WHAT MATTERS TO CHILDREN *touching the world, exploring how it works*

Big ideas:

form and function
fitness for purpose
adaptability
substitutes
diversity

INVESTIGATE variety in...

furniture in kitchens

fridge
toaster
balti dish
chapatti roller
wok
mincing machine
salad spinner
blender
cupboard racks

chairs
folding
revolving
fixed and portable
shooting stick
a milking stool
a nursing chair
a dentist's chair
wheelchairs
Van Gogh's chair

furniture in bedrooms

beds
single, double
King, Queen
cots and babies beds
bunk beds
camp beds
hammocks
four poster
fold out
futon
inflatable…

tables
their shapes
their number of
legs – 4, 1, 3, 0?
their purpose –
altar, airline tray,
desk, board room
their workings –
flaps, extension
leaves…

cupboards, wardrobes,
chest of drawers, dressers…
stairs and steps

*Have nothing in your houses that you do **not** know to be useful or **believe** to be beautiful.*
William Morris

Verbs
COLLECT
DISCUSS
VISIT
DRAW
DESIGN & MAKE
POLISH
COMPARE & CONTRAST
DECONSTRUCT
REASSEMBLE
EVALUATE
DECORATE
REDUCE & ENLARGE

VISIT
an auction room
a department store furniture department
factories   a church   studios
a museum   a banqueting hall
a narrow boat
a caravan   a gurdwara

Never forget...

…the child's interest in the concrete events of the physical world.
Susan Isaacs

INVESTIGATE
ways of making a table
bigger or smaller

ways of folding
furniture up small

ways of storing tiny
objects…huge
objects

Children, like poets, writers, musicians and scientists, are avid seekers and builders of images.
Loris Malaguzzi

FIND
the biggest…
the smallest…
the oldest…
the newest…
the easiest to make…
the most beautiful…

Questions worth asking

- Why are there so many kinds of beds, chairs, tables, cupboards?
- Why do cats and dogs have beds but not chairs or tables?
- What would you do if you didn't have any furniture?

DISCUSS the functions of furniture
…for sitting on, for sleeping on, for eating at, for going up and down, for working at, for relaxing in...

DISCUSS substitutes:
If you haven't got a clock/ladder/enough chairs use a…
My husband falls asleep in the bath.
My friend's baby slept in a chest of drawers.
I know someone who climbed up the library shelves to get to the books at the top.

Links with
First-hand experience:
what matters to children
V is for variety

Learning:
what matters to children
U is for learners thirst
for understanding

MAKE
design and make furniture for
kings and queens
a giant
a baby
a doll's house …
make the bed for the princess in *The Princess and the Pea*

Materials
what is furniture made of?
why? why not?
is it old or new?
precious or cheap?
hand made or mass produced?
decorated or plain?
shiny or soft?
outdoors or indoors?

Books for children
Billy Tibbles Moves Out! — Jan Fearnley
Peepo! — Janet and Allan Ahlberg
The Princess and the Pea — Traditional
The Three Bears — Traditional
Six Dinner Sid — Inga Moore
The Magic Bed — John Burningham
What! — Kate Lum and Adrian Johnson

Books for adults
Shoe and Metre — Reggio Children

F is for furniture: a learning story

Furniture studies

In a small one-class entry infant school in a large industrial city, the staff entered on a month long investigation of furniture. Each class took a different theme, focusing on a different aspect of this enormous topic.

Launderette furniture

To enrich the youngest children's domestic play, the educators in this class embarked on an investigation of launderette furniture. Some children had been playing with bubbles in the water tray. One child remarked, 'It's like a washing machine'. Another ran to the book box and found a story book with launderette washing machines on the front cover, called *The Frogs go on Holiday*. The children asked the teacher to read it aloud to them and when she did, one asked, 'Is there really such a thing as launderettes?' The very next day a small group set off to find out. They returned delighted with the proclamation, 'Launderettes are really, really real and they have LOADS of good things in them.' But what exactly? The next day another small group set off to investigate, What do launderettes have in them? They returned bursting with an answer, 'Machines… machines is what they have. All different ones. Washing machines, spinning machines, drying machines, money change machines, washing powder machines, big bag machines in case you've lost your big bag.'

While other delegations visited the launderette throughout the week to find out about launderette life, the remaining children set about recreating a launderette world by making launderette furniture. Within less than a week the corridor outside this part of the school (the class shared two large adjoining rooms) was transformed. A long row of washers and driers, created from a fine collection of cardboard boxes, stood on one side, and on the other, a row of chairs labelled with the name and logo of this flourishing establishment. They played launderettes in their newly created role play area. At most times of the day a group of mothers and fathers, with their babies in buggies, could be found sitting in the launderette, gossiping about their children's illnesses, the price of soap, the length of the wash cycle, or reading magazines and making shopping lists as they waited for their load to finish. Service washes were available and dry cleaning was taken in. Two busy employees checked in loads of washing, ticking off items and estimating prices and delivery times. There was often a great drama about a missing sock or shirt. When monsters or robbers appeared, they usually brought a bag of washing with them to put through a wash cycle, waiting patiently as true launderette customers do, before resuming their monster or robber behaviour.

F is for furniture

The rest of the school was organised into four parallel mixed age classes of five, six and seven year olds. The teachers consulted each other and decided on different approaches to the common enquiry, basing their choices on children's current interests and selecting a different curricular focus from their most recent whole class enquiry.

Folding furniture

Here the focus was on folding furniture. Day after day parents arrived at the classroom door with deck chairs, high chairs, camp beds, shooting sticks, camping tables and chairs, buggies, card tables, step ladders and more, much more. These objects were investigated, drawn and labelled and their working explained. Then the model making began, at first with art straws. But the children were soon dissatisfied with folding furniture that didn't fold properly. More problem solving. More attentive study of the deck chairs - the favourite items in the collection (despite the squeezed fingers and sticking plasters).

The Three Bears' furniture

This class of children were deeply into traditional fairy tales and so The Three Bears house was set up. The construction work was challenging. The task of building two chairs that would hold the children's weight and a third that would collapse to order, proved almost endlessly demanding, but was eventually mastered by the children. The beds were easier, thanks to Community Playthings. The kitchen furniture was no problem, and then the cooking could begin. The head teacher recorded in her log, ruefully, that she had NEVER eaten so much porridge.

On some days bears could be seen in the launderette, bringing a bag of washing to do while the porridge cooled down.

Six year old Millie chose chairs from her own home for each bear in the story .- but she won't say who is who!

F is for *furniture*

Kitchen furniture: a fridge

The class chose to investigate one aspect of kitchen furniture, the fridge. There were many expeditions to the fridge in the school cooking area, to take temperatures, to collect ice cubes for experiment and re-experiment. They spent a long time researching this interesting question: how many times will the same piece of ice melt and re-freeze? This enquiry was curtailed by the weary teacher after thirteen repeats. She urged the children to move on. A lost opportunity perhaps?

The fridge in the school kitchen was explored, measured, drawn and labelled, its contents inventoried and the school cook interviewed. The resourceful class teacher discovered a site in the city's industrial zone where discarded refrigerators were stored before being destroyed. She collected two specimens, one large and one small and brought them into the classroom. Children of course were instructed about the dangers of actually going inside a fridge. Much purposeful activity followed, as every constituent part of them was investigated, compared, contrasted and discussed. To conclude the project, the logic of things gave way to the logic of the imagination (see **T** is for thinking) and the children filled the refrigerators with 3D models of appropriate food: for a giant in the large fridge, and food for a witch in the small one. The green and slimy potions that filled the witch's fridge were unforgettable. Some of the parents were amused but not complacent. 'Wherever have the children seen such loathsome little green dishes before?' they wondered.

Office furniture

This was taught by two part-time teachers. They planned an enquiry into office furniture. One of them led the factual side of the project and small groups of children visited the school office to explore the mysteries of filing cabinets, word processors, revolving chairs, photocopiers and answer phones. They completed inventories and interviewed the office staff. They measured the time it took to word process a letter on the computer and the time it took to write one by hand. They discussed the reason for each item of furniture being in the office, and in the course of the discussion, worked on the big ideas of fitness for purpose and the relationship between form and function. They debated the question, 'What makes an office an office?' and concluded that it wasn't the furniture: what makes an office is the things that people do there.

The second teacher took charge of recreating an office in the classroom as a stimulus for office play. The children were especially delighted by the arrival in their classroom of a tall metal cabinet containing some wire clothes hangers and a broken umbrella… all kinds of stories resulted and the cabinet was soon full of clothes to match the characters in these stories. This part of the work culminated in the public performance of an office drama, scripted by the children, in two parts, though this was not at first announced. In the first part a stereotyped female secretary (meek, polite, and undemanding) was bullied by an equally stereotyped male boss (three piece pin striped suit). Before the head teacher could leap to her feet to point out the evils of this representation, (the whole school were working on an equity awareness project) the second part of the drama began and the two roles were reversed! The moral lesson became plain, especially to the humbled and contrite head teacher.

 **is for goats, guinea pigs, gerbils, giant African snails, goldfish and other gorgeous animals**

WHAT MATTERS TO CHILDREN *being with living things, finding out how to keep other living things safe*

Big ideas: **conservation**
care
protection
duty

DISCUSS
What is a pet?
Should animals be kept as pets? Why? Why not?
Why do people keep animals as pets?
Does it matter if animals smell?
What Lizzie, aged 11 said,
I really wanted to keep a pet snake, but my mum didn't want to keep dead mice in the freezer. Would it be okay for me to feed a pet snake mice, when my friend's pet is a mouse?

MAKE | **TELL SOMEONE**
your own | about a pet you have
animal stories | cared for or loved

Music
Carnival of the animals — Saint Saëns
The Cat's Duet — Giaochino Rossini
Mosquito Dance — Bela Bartòk

You can know the name of a bird in all the languages of the world, but when you're finished, you'll know absolutely nothing whatever about the bird... So let's look at the bird and see what it's doing - that's what counts. I learned very early the difference between knowing the name of something and knowing something. Richard Feynman

---

FIND OUT *about*
famous authors who have written stories about animals, and what inspired them

COLLECT
animal noises
make an animal noise symphony
animal commands
sit, heel, fetch, run, down boy, woah, giddeeup, walk on, walkies, come bye, away

MAKE a (three minute) film featuring your pet/an animal
direct it, or star in it, or operate the camera/phone/ipod

choose your genre:
fact, fiction, documentary

be involved in the editing process
find music to match the animal images

Invite an audience to see the finished films

Get involved with animals
take a dog for a walk
help to groom a horse
clean out your animal home
watch ducklings hatch
some people prefer to watch others handle animals.

Get involved in national pet month each April
visit *www.nationalpetmonth.org.uk* for more information, and useful advice on animals

---

Questions worth asking
What is the best way for animals to live?

INVESTIGATE
how animals move: centipedes, snails, frogs, caterpillars, blackbirds, wagtails, rabbits, tadpoles, ducklings...

INVESTIGATE
the feel of animals
smooth silky
rough soft
fluffy scaley
slimy wet...
make up your own
'animal feely' words
STITCH
'feel-it-samples' of animal textures.
Identify the animal they represent by the feel, not the look.

MAKE music for
a mouse
a giant African snail
a stick insect
a St. Bernard dog
a kitten
a horse
a foal

Links with
First-hand experience:
what matters to children
S is for surfaces
Learning:
what matters to children
N is for Nel Noddings:
learning to care

Visits and visitors
wildlife centre
zoos
farms
local stables
vet
animals in natural environments
a shepherd with a working dog
a pond teeming with tadpoles
a dog show
a puppy trainer
animal owners of different ages

Collaboratively agree the do's and don'ts of keeping animals.

Books for children
Animals in Art (Come Look with Me)
Gladys S. Blizzard
Black Beauty — Anna Sewell
Charlotte's Web — E.B. White
The Incredible Journey — Sheila Burnford
The Rabbit Problem — Julia Donaldson
The Wind in the Willows — Kenneth Grahame
Poems
Hurt No Living Thing — Christina Rosetti
Stopping by Woods on a Snowy Evening
Robert Frost

Books for adults
Happiness in Education — Nel Noddings

is for goats, guinea pigs, gerbils, giant African snails, goldfish and other gorgeous animals: learning stories

In this section we consider animals that children are likely to encounter as pets at home, on visits to farms, outdoors in general, and at sensory sessions in zoos and wildlife centres. (Some of them may even begin with **G**!)

Animals by
Donka age 5, Nazheen age 5, Pristee age 6, Bradley age 8, Kacper age 11

Animals on a grand scale: farms in schools

In a densely populated area of north London, a Children's Centre and Primary School share outdoor areas. This includes an on site farm yard, officially opened in May 2009. The farm is home to ducks, chickens, pigs, goats and rabbits animals. The Children's Centre prospectus proudly boasts to parents:

> Feathers at their little fingertips, galloping goats eating out of the palm of their hand, wiggling noses with our rabbits and toddling with our waddlers. Our little helpers may even get involved in collecting freshly laid eggs for sale to the local community. Making friends with our sociable brood in this powerful hands-on learning environment will help your child develop:
> • Responsible, caring and respectful ways
> • A wider variety of communication skills
> • A sense of pride, confidence and self-worth
> • Decision making and logical thinking.
> We provide a safe supervised setting. Allowing children to have some control, by actively feeding and nurturing the animals, ensures that they remain engaged with their learning environment whilst having lots of fun.

On the shared site, children from six months to 11 years of age spend time with the animals. Many school aged children are keen to volunteer to apply for positions of responsibility as committee members for the farm.

Animals are important: children need to encounter them.

Where?

How?

What do they do as a result of the experience?

And what do they learn?

 **G** is for **g**oats, **g**uinea pigs, **g**erbils, **g**iant African snails, **g**oldfish and other **g**orgeous animals: *learning stories*

Kacper age eleven

Sahil age nine

The pictures included in this chapter have been supplied by the school's art co-ordinator, collected from children who enjoy spending time closely observing their beloved farm animals, talking about them, feeling them, looking hard and listening, making sketches and taking photographs, all of which they used as a basis for their drawings.

is for goats, guinea pigs, gerbils, giant African snails, goldfish and other gorgeous animals: learning stories

Imari age six

Animals on a smaller scale: animals in books

Not every school is able, or even willing, to establish an on site farm such as the one described earlier. Many educators are, nevertheless, committed to ensuring that children regularly meet animals face to face. Some educators invite animals whenever it is relevant and possible - perhaps even just for a visit at story time.

Determined to give children first-hand experiences of animals, Lisa, a reception class teacher wasn't keen to be responsible for any full-time resident pets, but made some simple changes to her approach with children so that they regularly engaged with animals. She said,

> Since the *[First-hand experience]* conference day I've made changes. We always start each week with a book focus, but now we do this differently. Now we always think, 'How does this link with first-hand experience? What could we offer?' So recently we started from a book, *Tom Rabbit*, and I made sure there was a real rabbit in the classroom.

Lisa went on to continue to develop opportunities for offering real life experiences in association with books, which often involved bringing animals into school.

After hearing about Lisa's practice, Marie a teacher of eight year olds, who were reading the classic J.M. Barrie story, Peter Pan, decided to invite a friend to bring his full grown St. Bernard into the classroom. On the day of the visit children were very struck by the size of it and the way it moved; none had ever seen such a big dog before. They felt how solid it was, how thick, long and shiny its fur was, how dribbly and drooly its mouth was, how warm its breath was, how noisy its breathing was, and how deep its bark. Some were struck by how happy and docile the very VERY big dog seemed, as they thought such a large dog might be fierce or aggressive. One child said, 'What big eyes you have, Bernie,' remembering Red Riding Hood's encounter with a wolf.

Just as Lisa's class of children had enjoyed the pure 'rabbitness' of rabbit, these children encountered the very 'doggyness' of this huge dog, and had a much better understanding of the power that the dog Nana commanded in Barrie's story.

 **H** is for homes

WHAT MATTERS TO CHILDREN *having a sense of big belonging, being with people who care about me*

Background

During the writing of this new edition, the authors discussed **H** is for homes, and whether it should have a place. We considered the diversity of children's home lives and the wide spectrum of homes children live in. We thought about what constitutes a home, children living in luxury homes, having second (or third) homes for holiday and pleasure, having no home at all or living in conditions of poverty, children who may have lost their home through financial problems, or through conflict in their home country, children living in temporary homes, living as refugees, or asylum seekers. We also considered the increasing number of children who have more than one home base, living part-time with each parent and often grandparents too.

We agreed that the subject of homes threw up many difficult questions. While we do not want to avoid difficult questions (see **Q** is for questions), we seriously considered removing the **H** is for homes chapter. We thought that the subject is so vast and raises such serious and sometimes sensitive issues, we would not be able to do it justice here. But we changed our minds…

Big ideas:

diversity
fitness for purpose
shelter and protection
safety and comfort
survival and luxury

Can schools be like homes?

Visiting a school in Iceland, from the minute I set foot inside, I was impressed by the homely atmosphere all through the building. I wondered what made it so?
I noticed...
- the ages of children were from 6 to 16
- each class had its own single toilet with a door you could lock
- no one wore shoes; everyone wore slippers, including the teachers.

Mole and Ratty are out in the Wild Wood late at night.

[Mole] stopped dead in his tracks … Home!...those invisible little hands pulling and tugging all one way! … his old home that he had hurriedly forsaken... Now with a rush of old memories how clearly it stood up before him, in the darkness! Shabby indeed and poorly furnished, and yet his, the home he had made for himself, the home he had been so happy to get back to after his day's work. And the home had been happy with him, too, evidently, and was missing him, and wanted him back, and was telling him so, through his nose, sorrowfully, reproachfully, but with no bitterness or anger; only with plaintive reminder that it was there, and wanted him… 'Please stop, Ratty!' pleaded the poor Mole, in anguish of heart. 'You don't understand! It's my home, my old home!...'

From *Wind in the Willows*, Kenneth Graham p286-7

Questions worth asking

- What makes a home a home?
- What's the difference between a house and a home?

LOOK AT homes in art

Dutch interiors	Pieter de Hooch
Interior and Landscape	Utagawa Toyaharu
Ndebele painted houses	
Tar Beach II	Faith Ringgold
The Cottage Home	William Snape
The Doctor	Luke Fildes
The Potato Eaters	Vincent Van Gogh
Victorian Interior	Horace Pippin

VISIT a variety of places where people live

attic flat   basement flat   bungalow   caravan   houseboat   lighthouse   mansion   mobile home   palace   penthouse   residential home   tree house

Links with

First-hand experience:
what matters to children
K is for **keys**

Learning:
what matters to children
B is for learners belong to a community of learners

MAKE
a tree house
a crooked house
a den
a home for a teddy

LOOK AT
a spider's web
(is it a home?)

INVESTIGATE
a bird's nest
(is it a home?)

MAKE
clay bricks

FIND OUT
about animal homes

PHOTOGRAPH
a variety of places where people live and make an exhibition of the photos

Books for children

Charlie's House	Reviva Shermbrucker
Hansel and Gretel	Jane Ray
Hansel and Gretel	Anthony Browne
Ndebele	Margaret Courtney Clarke
Lost and Found	Oliver Jeffers
The Colour of Home	Mary Hoffmann
The Mousehole Cat	Antonia Barber
The Tree of Cranes	Allen Say
The Wizard of Oz	Frank L. Baum

Poems

The Blue Room	Richard Edwards

Books for adults

The Home-Maker	Dorothy Canfield Fisher
Love is Not Enough	Bruno Bettelheim

H is for homes: learning stories

Is a spider's web a home?

In a small group in a class of five and six year olds, one boy asked a question totally unrelated to the activity they were engaged in: 'Is a spider's web a home?'

The educator said nothing, but waited to see how the children in the group would answer. At first they seemed to ignore his question, but soon came up with Spiderman related comments.

'Spiderman makes webs.'

'He shoots them like this [making Spiderman actions.'

'Yeah he catches all the baddies. He traps them in his webs.'

The boy who had asked the original question came back with, 'Yeah, but I'VE seen a REAL spider's web AND A REAL spider was making it.'

'But Spiderman makes real webs too.'

'No. Only spiders. Spiderman's not real, so how can he make real webs?'

'Well he DOES. And spiders don't. It's only Spiderman who can make webs…
(he pondered) DO spiders make webs? DO they?'

'They do, I watched one in my house, but I don't know if they actually live in their webs, so are spider's webs homes?'

'But how do they make the webs? Do they shoot them out like Spiderman? HOW do they do it?'

The teacher asked, 'Simon, have you ever seen a real spider's web?'

'A REAL spider's web? A Spiderman's web? In my video Spiderman makes the webs.'

There were now clearly two things to investigate. The next steps were obvious.

Settling in to an additional home

Six year old Charlie's parents have recently separated. Three weeks ago he started living in two places, one part-time in a house with his mother, where he's lived since he was six months old, and the other, part-time with his father in a new flat.

Picking Charlie up from school on parent-change-over-day, Charlie's father told him to be ready... he had set up a treasure hunt at the flat with mystery clues for Charlie to follow a trail and find a treasure. His father wanted to help Charlie learn his way around this new unfamiliar space, so he would quickly feel at home there. The trail led Charlie to all manner of places in the flat; he was proud when he realised how much he already knew about the layout and where the crockery and utensils were to be found. Charlie enjoyed the mystery and excitement, solving simple clues to find out where to go next.

is for 'I' the active learner

WHAT MATTERS TO CHILDREN *From birth, children know what's important to them.*
This book takes 'what matters to children' as the basis for proposing ways in which their fascination with the world and the people in it, can be encouraged, extended and deepened.

This is another of the pages that are different from the others. Here we expand on some of the thinking that lies behind the whole book and that underpins our argument: young children need active, first-hand experiences to feed and exercise their growing human powers.

The problem as we see it

- continuing and growing pressures on early years and primary educators – levels, standards, outcomes, pace and delivery

- a resulting loss of freedom for both children and their educators

- over-prescription of curriculum, activities and experiences

- a resulting proliferation of second-hand experiences – paper and pencil, internet, computer images, tablets, iPads, mobile phones and things yet to come…

The alternative

- reinstate children as powerful agents in their own learning

- reinstate children's access to the real, meaningful, living world

- reactivate children's capacity to act for themselves

I AM

From birth children tell us of their

essential being…

I AM, I FEEL, I SUFFER, I LOVE, I REACH OUT, I TOUCH, I EXPLORE, I EXPERIMENT, I MAKE MEANING, I DESIRE TO UNDERSTAND.

I AM becomes I CAN

As children grow so do their powers to act on the world…

I CAN... touch it, taste it, prod it, eat it, adapt it, move about in it, explore it

I CAN   think about it

I CAN   share it with my friends

I CAN   ask questions about it

I CAN   show you what fascinates me

AND SO I LEARN:

Bit by bit to know and understand the lovely and difficult world – and all the things that matter to me.

IT'S IMPORTANT TO ME!

to act
touching and tasting the world
moving about in it
making a mark on it
finding out how to keep safe in it
making my own map of it
making collections

to explore
what is in the world
who is in it
who am I
what is it made of
how it works

to be
being with friends
being in different places
being with living things
being with people who
care about me

to understand
knowing the world
making sense of it
having a sense of big belonging
understanding how it works
how it works
making my own moral map

is for I *the active learner*: **WISE WORDS ABOUT CHILDREN**

The view of children as active learners that we are putting forward on these pages is not a new invention. Classic texts about children, schools and learning are full of powerful expressions of this very theme; contemporary writers continue to emphasise the same idea.

The child who is learning by doing is learning many things besides the one thing he is supposed to be learning. He is learning to desire, to purpose, to place, to initiate, to execute: he is learning to profit by experience, to think, to reason, to judge.
Edmond Holmes

In order to be creative, a child needs not only the opportunity but also the capacity, the power to make a choice.
Christian Schiller

No sticks or carrots needed...

Rather than asking 'What stick or carrot will make the children active in certain ways?' or 'what will make them go in this direction rather than that?' we would do well to turn the problem round and to say: children will go in any case, for it is an expression of their being to be purposeful and energetic.

R. A. Hodgkin

It is not what we do to the child or for the child that educates him, but what we enable him to do for himself, to see and learn and feel and understand for himself. The child grows by his own efforts and his own real experience.
Susan Isaacs

(We have) a highly optimistic view of the child; a child who possesses many resources at birth, and with an extraordinary potential which has never ceased to amaze us; a child with the independent means to build up his or her own thoughts, ideas, questions and attempts at answers; with a high level of competence in conversing with adults, the capacity to observe things and reconstruct them in their entirety. This is a gifted child, for whom we need a gifted teacher.
Loris Malaguzzi

 **is for joining**

WHAT MATTERS TO CHILDREN *what the world is made of, how the world works*

Big ideas:

form and function
diversity
fitness for purpose

INVESTIGATE
a skeleton
a skull
a bicycle
a pair of scissors
an estuary
the horizon
how many joins in a door? a book?
how many hinges in a kitchen?
find some things with no joins in them
unravel some knitting
patchwork

USE
all of the tools below for useful projects

Toolbox
bulldog clips   buttons   chains
crochet hooks   duct tape   elastic bands
glue   glue guns   hammer
nails and screws   needle and thread
paper clips   pins   pliers
screw drivers   sellotape   split pins
stapler   string   tapes
treasury tags   zips…

MAKE
a daisy chain
a human chain
books with stitched pages, zigzag books…
jigsaw puzzles
a box with a hinge
a railway with junctions

DISCUSS
Some useful joins and joints (legs,
holding hands, a bicycle chain)
All the different ways of joining clothes…

MAKE
Superman's cloak
Robin Hood's green tabard
Cinderella's ragged dress/ball gown
Max's Wolf suit…
then...

FIND OUT
which is the best way to fasten them

Links with
First-hand experience: what matters to children
F is for furniture

Learning: what matters to children
J is for learners do joined up learning

COLLECT
mechanical toys
jointed toys
stitched toys

VISIT
a joiner at work
a dressmaker
at work
a railway junction

SKETCH

PHOTOGRAPH

OBSERVE

DOCUMENT

INTERVIEW
PEOPLE

Questions worth asking
Why do some joins move and some not?
Why is some writing joined up?

OBSERVE
how blackberries join onto a bush
how sweet peas join onto a trellis
how doors join onto walls
how feathers join onto birds
how fingers join onto hands
how goose grass joins onto socks and trousers
how hands join together
how sleeves join onto jackets
how Virginia creeper joins onto a pergola
   or wall
how Velcro fastens shoes
how zips work

Books for children
A Most Unusual Lunch — Robert Bender
The Invention of Hugo Cabret — Brian Selznick
Little Cloud — Eric Carle
Over the Steamy Swamp — Paul Geraghty
The Great Big Enormous Turnip — Alexei Tolstoy
The Peach Tree — Norman Pike
The Little Boat — Kathy Henderson

Books for adults
The Last Runaway — Tracey Chevalier

J is for joining: learning story

Joining with the past: stitching costumes

Children aged four to eleven years attending a small rural school worked together to learn about life in Tudor England. Their studies included architecture, the language and literature of the time, music, dance and food, and costume. This last was particularly important as the project would conclude with a visit to Kentwell Hall in Suffolk for a day when they would step back into the past. For this they needed costumes so they designed and made their own; dyeing, cutting and sewing each one.

First they dyed cloth, making natural dyes from onion skins and nettles; they then made patterns for their costumes: tabards, underskirts and headscarves for the girls, tunics and hoods for the boys. Once the pieces were cut, the children were ready to stitch. It was tempting to use a sewing machine but this was Tudor England. With painstaking care each child hand-stitched their costume, including shoes: felt shoes for the younger children, leather for those who could manage the tough material, the curved needle and waxed thread.

Accompanied by parents and younger siblings, some of them babies, also dressed in Tudor attire, the children travelled to Kentwell Hall where they stepped through a time tunnel, walking from one Elizabethan age to another.

Exploring joining

An early years unit used a range of approaches to explore the properties of joining. Their planning reflected the way in which the educators at this unit matched *First-hand experience: what matters to children* with the Foundation Stage early learning goals. On the weekly planning sheet the educators identified key learning objectives. These were matched to first-hand experiences that would enrich the learning selected from the page J *is for joining*.

The children linked their bodies in movement sessions, twisting, rolling, and making arches, climbing under and over linked hands to make different patterns. They also used parachute games to develop their awareness of space and to work cooperatively with others.

In the construction area the children joined wood and card using a range of tools and techniques to investigate fixed, moveable and hinged joints. The children built car and railway tracks and a variety of forms of transport using large cardboard boxes linked together using string, rope or card, and towers from construction kits. In this way the children learned to compare sizes, to name shapes and to consider questions such as,

Which building wobbles the most?
Why do you think this is?
How does this joint work?
Would these joints work with cardboard boxes?

They learned through first-hand experience the meaning of joint, hinge, strong, fixed, moveable, arch, stretch, flexible, rigid, transport, push and pull.

Outdoors, in the rain, the children played with gutters supported on boxes to send plastic ducks down the tubes. They explored questions such as:

Did the ducks travel more quickly than the cars?
Is water a better means of transport than wheels?
How long can we make the chute and does it make a difference?'

The story of *The Enormous Turnip* was read and retold by the children using story box characters. The children made their own books to write their versions of the story, learning ways to join pages and chapters together, and using joining words such as 'then', 'next', 'later',
'afterwards'' and 'but'.

At the end of the enquiry the educators looked back at their planning sheets and were surprised and delighted at the unexpected and valuable learning that had taken place. The achievements of the children surpassed the early learning goals identified on the planning sheets. The learning had been richer, deeper and completely engaging.

 **is for knowing**

WHAT MATTERS TO CHILDREN *In these kinds of knowing, children come to understand the issues that matter most to them –being in the world, exploring the world, acting on the world, understanding how it works*

This alphabet page is another that differs from most of the others. On these pages we offer some suggestions about the kinds of knowing that matter most to children. We have become very familiar with long lists of the things that children are expected to know and understand at certain ages. We recognise the importance of this kind of knowing in children's education. The relation of letters to sounds, the conventions of written English, the vocabulary of addition and subtraction, telling the time, multiplication tables, months of the year: of course all this knowledge is important. But there are other kinds of knowing that are just as significant for children's intellectual development, especially:

KNOWING HOW

KNOWING WHERE

KNOWING WHEN

KNOWING WHO

KNOWING WHY

Links with

Learning: *what matters to children*
K is for children know more than adults think they do

Children are always ready to shake the tree of knowledge.

Loris Malaguzzi

Since we cannot know what knowledge will be most needed in the future, it is senseless to try to teach it in advance. Instead we should try to turn out people who love learning so much and who learn so well that they will learn whatever needs to be learned

John Holt

Books for children

A Ladder to the Stars	Simon Puttock
Drop Dead!	Babette Cole
Goodbye Mog	Judith Kerr
It Can't be True: incredible visual comparisons	Rob Houston
Supposing	Frances Thomas and Ross Collins
Susan Laughs	Jeannie Willis and Tony Ross
Tell Me Again About the Night I Was Born	Jamie Lee Curtis
When Hitler Stole Pink Rabbit	Judith Kerr

Books for adults

I am Malala	Malala Yousafzai
Huckleberry Finn	Mark Twain
A Kestrel for a Knave	Barry Hines

 **is for knowing**

KNOWING HOW

to look after myself [feeding - dressing – planning – exploring] – how to ask for help – how to help someone else – to use tools safely – to find out how things work

KNOWING WHO

are my companions – who I can trust – who sets the boundaries that keep me safe – who trusts me – who will help me – who I can help – who is in charge

KNOWING WHERE

my important people go when they go away – where I can go on my own – where I am safe – where I can go with someone else – where I can find things – where things live – where I can't go

KNOWING WHEN

some things happen regularly – some things happen without any warning – when things go wrong, they will get better – when I can decide for myself – when other people will decide for me – when I can choose – what's going to happen when – what's going to happen next – knowing when it's important to be quiet

KNOWING WHY

sometimes I have to do as I am told – why I feel so many different feelings [joyful, miserable, furious, anxious, loving, rebellious…] – why other people's feelings change too

Being in the world

On this page we suggest some of the important things about the world and the other people in it that children really **do** want to know. We believe that, given the right support, children **can** know all these things, with confidence, because they matter so much. But children do not come by these ways of knowing all at once, or at specific ages. Coming to know oneself, and one's being in the world is a long, slow process. As children engage in this process, they are working on the life-long project of understanding some very big ideas indeed.

Big ideas:

CAUSE and EFFECT
TIME, MYSTERY, IDENTITY,
RECIPROCITY, MORAL RESPONSIBILITY
LIFE and DEATH

(In the nursery school) the children are free to explore and experiment with the physical world, the way things are made, the fashion in which they break and burn, the properties of water and gas and electric light, the rain, the sunshine, the wind and the frost. The teacher is there to (bring) together the material and the situations which may give children the means of answering their own questions about the world.

Susan Isaacs

 **is for listening and looking**

On this page we argue that every first-hand activity engaged in by children involves looking and listening of some kind, sometimes many kinds. The educator's responsibility is to make sure the conditions are totally supportive of worthwhile looking and listening. The most important thing to remember is that worthwhile looking and listening take time. None of us, whatever our age, can look or listen properly if we are being hurried. We need plenty of time to use these simple ways of making sense of our experience, and, what's more, we need plenty of time to talk about what we see and hear. Children's looking and listening are no different, but they depend on their educators to provide the time and the space they require.

Worthwhile looking means:

taking it slowly
talking about what you see
looking again and again
looking at details
looking for surprises
talking about what you see
looking for what is missing
looking and comparing
looking near and looking far
looking at everything
talking about what you see
looking at one thing at a time
looking at new things, animals, plants
talking about what you see
looking at mysterious things
looking at the real thing, not an image of it
looking at pain
looking at beauty
talking about what you see
looking at turbulence
looking at harmony
looking with your hands as well as your eyes
talking about what you see

Worthwhile listening means:

taking it slowly
talking about what you hear
asking questions, not just answering them
listening to yourself
listening to your friends
talking about what you hear
listening to everybody's ideas
listening to everybody's stories
listening to their discoveries
listening to their meanings
talking about what you hear
listening to difference
listening to agreement
listening to debate and discussion
talking about what you hear
listening to objections
listening to complaints
listening with an open heart
talking about what you hear – not the sounds,
but the meanings

Children use all the senses they have for looking and listening.

L *is for* listening and looking

THE CHINESE CHARACTER

The Chinese character for listening is made up of four different characters all of which are involved in the work of listening.

EAR	EYE
BRAIN	HEART

In a mixed Year 5/6 classroom in a multi-ethnic inner city primary school, this Chinese character and commentary were displayed in a prominent place. A researcher visiting the school to document the class teacher's deep understanding of children's learning asked her to explain its significance. She described how it was connected to what she sees as the inescapable emotional dimension of learning, how she seeks to engage children in their learning with energy and passion, with hearts as well as brains. So listening, as a part of learning, is equally a work of the heart; in her words:

We talk about where the heart comes into this, if you are not listening properly to somebody, you can't feel the emotion in their words, so you can't respond in the way that you should.

(Hart et al. 2004:89)

RE-PRESENTATION

In the Italian region of Reggio Emilia, educators often use a technique they call '␣re-presentation'. They document children's talk, which they take very seriously, whenever they are listening and looking together. Later, they work as a group, using the notes of their talk to identify ideas and comments they would like to explore and extend. After their shared discussion, they 're-present' these promising ideas to the children, inviting them to say more, to debate with each other and their educators, to take their thinking and learning to a deeper level.

Books for educators

Adventuring in Early Childhood Education	Robin Duckett and Mary Jane Drummond
A Story of Smallness and Light	Deb Wilenski
A Study of Imagination in Early Childhood	Ruth Griffiths
Dialogues with Children	Gareth Matthews
Listening to Four Year Olds	Jacqui Cousins
Listening to Young Children: The Mosaic Approach	Alison Clarke and Peter Moss
The Genius of Play	Sally Jenkinson

 **M** is for **mixing**

WHAT MATTERS TO CHILDREN *touching and tasting the world, exploring how things work*

Big ideas:

**identifying
naming
classifying
combining
change**

Where drawing may be the string quartet of art, the richness of painting is nearer to being a symphony. Rob Barnes

LOOK FOR well known mixtures
a rainbow
hundreds and thousands
sweet and sour   salt and vinegar
Cornish pasty filling
rice and peas   coleslaw
bread and butter pudding

COLLECT ingredients for making magic spells
a spell to make you blue
a spell to make you happy
a spell to make you small

Questions worth asking
- What is a mixture?
- What mixtures can you un-mix?
- How can you un-mix sounds?

Toolbox
blender brush cocktail shaker
filters and sieves   food processor
ice-cream maker loom mincer
palette knife   pestle and mortar
sound mixing desk spatula
spirtle whisk

INVESTIGATE
mixing with water
shampoo, dried fruit, paint, jelly, oil, ice, herbs, bicarbonate of soda

mixing sounds
instruments that make quiet, loud, sudden, continuous sounds
COMBINING sounds to make music that makes you think of the sea, a storm, wind, rain
MAKE a musical score of your composition
USE the score to replay your music

mixing voices
SING in harmony
SING a round

mixing smells
MAKE a cocktail of smells from water, leaves, grass, flowers, soil, and other natural materials…
COMPARE perfumes

mixing mud and compost
MAKE a compost heap
WAIT until it has decayed and use it in the garden

LIST
compound words (two whole words combined)
skyscraper, suitcase, snowflake, armchair, birthday, portmanteau, whiteboard, handkerchief
portmanteau words (two words run together)
chocoholic, brunch, motel, labradoodle, guestimate, mimsy
colour mixture words
purple, orange, brown, beige, green, turquoise, pink, mauve, grey, murple

INVESTIGATE
mixing colours
mixing paint
twisting yarns for weaving, stitching, making tapestry
overlaying cellophane, net, tissue paper, coloured acetates
dyeing cloth, batik, tie and dye
blending pastels, crayons
mixing flavours
breads, ice-cream, biscuits, cakes, jams, drinks, soups, sandwich fillings, curries, muesli, teas…

MAKE a role play area for
a fancy dress shop   an Indian restaurant
a perfume factory   an artist's studio
a painter and decorator   a bakery

Books for children
A Million Chameleons	James Young
In the Night Kitchen	Maurice Sendak
Pretend Soup: and Other Real Recipes	Mollie Katzen and Ann Henderson
The Giant Jam Sandwich	John Vernon Lord
The Mixed Up Chameleon	Eric Carle
The Magnificent I Can Read Music Book	Kate Petty and Jenny Maizels
The Periodic Table: elements with style	Adrian Dinglo and Simon Basher

Books for adults
Three Good Things	Hugh Fearnley Whittingstall
The Periodic Table	Primo Levi

VISIT
a recording studio
a bakery
a concrete mixer in use

THINK about these words
combination
collection
pollution
overlay
blend
filter

Links with
First-hand experience: *what matters to children*   **C** is for colourful curriculum

Learning: *what matters to children* **J** is for learners do joined up learning

Mixing to raise money

In a small rural village a group of children aged eight to twelve decided that the playground equipment on the recreation ground was no longer fit for their purpose; it was designed for younger children.

Having discussed this with the Parish Council, they researched catalogues to find something suitable and settled on a set of swing bars. These they thought would give them scope for action and were not too expensive: £369. They knew this would not be the final cost; in addition they would need a safety surface and there would be a charge for installation.

They set about making plans to raise the necessary funds.

Their first event was to have a stall at the village fete. They designed four games, ran the event and raised £70. They were on the way.

Their next plan was to hold a village 'Bake-Off'. Their list of classes reflected their enjoyment and experience of baking: cheese straws, chocolate brownies, a decorated cupcake, Easter nests, best cookie flavour, bread rolls in any shape, scones and a Victoria sponge. They chose eight adult classes: a loaf of bread, hot cross buns, a gluten-free fruit loaf, shortbread, Swiss roll, a Simnel cake and a Victoria sponge. There would be a small fee for entry and after judging the cakes would be sold.

There was much to do: posters and flyers to generate village interest, certificates to design and print, recipes to find and practice. The children weighed, measured, mixed and kneaded. The Parish Council was impressed. At their next meeting they passed a resolution to pay the balance. The children would have their equipment before they outgrew it!

Mixing garden cocktails

I planned the following investigation for my class of four to six year olds. It was one of four mini projects within the 'mixing' theme – mixing garden cocktails; mixing paint; mixing food; investigating things that don't mix.

I allocated an afternoon for each mini project over the space of a week, with a view to adapting my planning to respond to the children's interests. As a whole class, we talked about mixing smells from the garden in our outdoor area. To investigate further, we went on a class walk around the school grounds to collect suitable things we could add to our cocktails. The children found materials such as leaves, grass, petals and mud.

I provided some water and jars. The children selected the natural objects they wanted to mix together and spent over an hour mixing up their cocktails. Some revised their ideas as they were going along; removing and adding various things until their cocktail was just right. Most gave their mixture a name and enjoyed smelling each other's cocktails.

'I'm making perfume.'

'It smells like perfume.'

'Smell mine. It smells like ginger beer.'

'How do you make perfume?'

'You mix water and petals and grass and things.'

'The mud's all mixed in now.'

'I'm pretending mine's baby milkshake.'

'It smells like seawater.'

 **is for mixing: learning stories**

A frog study: mixing your own colour

In a nursery classroom Simon sat alone at a table. He'd come in from outside where he had just been looking at the pond and asking about frogs.

Where are the frogs?

Why aren't there any frogs here today?

Where do frogs go when they aren't here?

Simon remembered that he'd got a frog picture in a book and went inside to find it, but instead he started to gather tools for mixing powder paint. He got a palette and spoon, and some white, yellow and blue paint. He spooned a little white paint into the palette and looked at it. He spooned some yellow paint on top of the white and reached for a brush. He mixed the yellow and white powder together. He looked at the new pale yellow. He added a tiny amount of blue and mixed it. He looked at the mixture and smiled, then continued with the blue paint for some time. Next Simon reached for more yellow, loading the powder onto the spoon. As his arm hovered above the new green mix, he faltered and some yellow powder floated down, making tiny spots on the green. He paused and looked delighted, studying the paint for some time, before shouting out to everyone triumphantly,

'I've done it, I've done it. I've made Speckled Frog Green.
AND IT'S A REALLY GOOD ONE TOO!'

Can you un-mix water?

A class of 10 and 11 year olds was studying the school wildlife pond. They were worried about the water; it wasn't clear, it was a thick murky green. This gave rise to a discussion: shouldn't they live in clear water? (Was this water fit for wildlife?)

The children investigated ways of clearing the algae with pond plants and straw and over time they noticed an improvement, it did become clearer. Meanwhile further questions had arisen: how can water be clarified? Could they design a filter system? Would the water then be fit to drink?

The children entered into this with great enthusiasm, enlisting the support of their parents. Some wonderful machines were built using a variety of filtration materials: felt, gravel, sand, cotton, hessian, fragments of fleece gathered from fence posts, layered in re-purposed lemonade bottles. They mixed very muddy water to pour into each machine and compared the results. The water was definitely clearer; every machine was an effective filter, although there were degrees of clarity. But the children decided, (with strong support from their educators) that drinking the water was not an option.

M is for **mixing**

Millie mixes paint

Mixing fat balls for birds

At his nursery, Aiden used to mix seeds and fat to make fat balls for hanging outside to feed birds in winter.

He used yogurt pots as a mould, and added string so that they could be hung up when the mixture solidified.

Now eight, Aiden is interested in birds and proud to be a junior member of the RSPB. He has a bird feeder close to his bedroom window and watches birds from his room, using binoculars. He also goes on regular bird watching walks with his father and recognises a variety of different species. Sometimes Aiden visits a bird hide in Suffolk, with other young birdwatchers.

Aiden still makes bird seed feeders in the same way.

Sophie age six   *Donka age five*

 **N** is for night sky

WHAT MATTERS TO CHILDREN *being in different places, moving about in the world*

Big ideas: distance
vastness
infinity

Toolbox

telescopes   star maps   a planetarium
torches   reference books

What do Mary Hoffman and Jane Ray (1998) mean when they say,
The sky is a vast storybook open above us.
and
For thousands of years it also provided the most reliable map there was.

The greater cats with golden eyes
Stare out between the bars
Deserts are there and different skies
And night with different stars
Vita Sackville West

FIND constellations at different times of the year, wherever you are

The Plough
Orion
The Great Bear
Cassiopeia
The Pleiades
Your own star sign...

(you can use an Ipad app. to see which planets, constellations can be seen in the sky any night of the year)

INVESTIGATE

the sky at night in summer and winter - what can you see, imagine, name, discover?

VISIT

places to see the night sky
a planetarium
an observatory
the Science Museum, London and similar
(or borrow a portable planetarium)

meet an astronomer
meet a space scientist

Go for a night time walk when there is
a full moon
a new moon
a harvest moon
no moon...

MUSIC

Starry Starry Night   Don MacLean
The Planets   Gustav Holst

COLLECT different names for the same constellation

the Plough, the Dipper, the Pan Handle, the Ladle, Ursa Major, the Great Bear...
Make up alternative names for other constellations

MAKE

Your own constellations in the night sky and name them.
Can you see them every time you check?

Questions worth asking

🌿 Why is the moon broken today?
  (from Annabelle Dixon's questions book)
🌿 Which star do I have to stand on to see dinosaurs on the earth?
🌿 What does a star sound like?
🌿 Where does space end?
🌿 What is the universe?
🌿 How many stars are there?
🌿 Did you see that shooting star

AT NIGHT USE

a telescope   a star map...   all your senses

Stay up to date with night sky events- meteor showers, planetary line ups, satellite flight paths, comet passing nearby and become a regular sky watcher.

Books for children

Black Holes and stuff	Glen Murphy
How to Catch a Star	Oliver Jeffers
I See the Moon	Erika Mitton and Erik Pal
The Astrological Zodiac for Children	Rayne Storm
The Blackest Hole in Space	Penny Little and Vincent Vilga
The Sea of Tranquillity	Mark Haddon
The Story of Cassiopeia: A Roman Constellation (and others in the series)	Thomas Kingsley Troupe
Zoo in the Sky	Jacqueline Mitton and Christina Balit
100 Things to Spot in the Night Sky	Spotters Guides

Books for adults

Wonders of the Universe	Brian Cox and Andrew Cohen

Keep a moon diary

Sleep under the stars

NIGHT IN ART

Starry Night
Vincent Van Gogh

LOOK FOR

Venus and Jupiter,
Mars and Mercury
Spot a shooting star
on August 12th

Links with

First-hand experience: what matters to children   **O** is for out and about
Learning: what matters to children   **A** is for learners learn all the time

is for night time

WHAT MATTERS TO CHILDREN *moving about in the world, being in different places*

Big ideas:

change
security
time
cycles
light and dark
presence and
absence
rhythm

Toolbox

hand held torches and head torches, candles, lanterns, sleeping bags, bedtime stories, lullabies and night songs, blankets and pegs for making places dark, recording equipment to record the sounds of night…

On the night you were born,
the moon smiled with such wonder
the stars peeked in to see you
and the wind night whispered,
'Life will never be the same.'

Because there had never been anyone like you…
Ever in the world.

Nancy Tilman

Tell a bed time story- or listen to one

MAKE a dark place
GO FOR a night time walk
VISIT a familiar place after dark
Have a sleep-over - at a friends house, at a relatives house, in your school at night!
BUILD a camp fire
SPEND an evening without using any electric lights or lights with bulbs in…

INVESTIGATE

nocturnal animals
the noises of night
working at night
why do we have curtains at night?
how to make things show up when there is less light

VISIT

familiar places outdoors at night time
a place to find and hear nocturnal animals
a place to smell night scented stock
a supermarket at night

DISCUSS

why things are scary at night
why things are exciting at night

MUSIC

Peter Grimes	Benjamin Britten
A Midsummer Night's Dream	Felix Mendelssohn
Nocturne	John Field

MAKE

a night time den   a comfy bed
a midnight feast
sing a lullaby
tell a bedtime story to help someone sleep
make them up, or use ones you know

All education comes from experience. But not all experiences are genuinely or equally educative. So the task is to find the right experiences, which do not arrest or restrict the growth of further experience.

John Dewey

Questions worth asking

- What makes night night?
- Is night a beginning, an end, or a middle?
- Is midnight late today or early tomorrow?
- How do you know it's night if you haven't got a window or a clock?
- Do babies know when it's night?
- Why do birds wake me in the morning?
- Do sheep ever stop bleating at night?
- Where do my dreams come from?

AT NIGHT USE

a head torch a candle a lantern a tent
reflective clothing a whistle… all your senses

Books for children

Arabian Nights (illustrated version)	Anna Milbourne
A Midsummer Night's Dream	Andrew Matthew and William Shakespeare
A Mad Summer Night's Dream	Ruth Brown
In the Middle of the Night	Kathy Henderson
Imagine a Night	Rob Gonsalves
Just a Dream	Chris van Allsberg
Night Monkey, Day Monkey	Julia Donaldson
On the Night You Were Born	Nancy Tilman
The Boy and the Cloth of Dreams	Jenny Koralek
The Owl Who Was Afraid of the Dark	Jill Tomlinson

Poems

Bed in Summer	Robert Louis Stevenson
A Pocketful of Stars: poems about the night	Nikki Siegen-Smith

Books for adults

Blindness	Jose Saramago

NIGHT IN ART

Nocturne in Blue
Whistler

Most glorious night!
Thou wert not sent
for slumber.

Lord Byron

RECALL

sleep and dreams
night time memories

According to Jewish tradition a new day begins at nightfall.

Links with

First-hand experience: *what matters to children*   **O** is for out and about
Learning: *what matters to children*   **A** is for learners learn all the time

 is for night: learning stories

School sleep overs

In an effort to keep school trip costs down and make trips accessible for more children, ideally all of them, one primary school sets up regular sleep over nights in school - summer nights, spring nights, wintry dark nights. Sometimes trips are for small groups of children, and sometimes they involve a whole class or year group. For outdoor nights they use one of the central quadrangle areas, surrounded by the school hall and classrooms. Here they set up their tents. For indoor sleepover nights they use the school hall, but some children want to set up sleeping dens in their own classrooms and, at their suggestion, this is gone on the agenda for the school council to discuss as an option for next time.

Camping nights usually include a campfire, songs around it and toasting marshmallows, and outdoor games late into the evening on summer nights. Indoor nights usually involve bedtime story telling sessions, singing lullabies and playing 'help-to-get to-sleep games' led by children and adults. A favourite indoor night time activity is torchlight dances, using the ceiling of the school hall.

Planning how to get to sleep

Children in each tent made pre-plans for how to get to sleep if they were having difficulty. Angelina and Clare, two good friends made these rules:

Tell each other stories.
No talking or giggling after 9.30 …or 10.00.
Play an alphabet game in your head
or quietly with one person near you.
Stay calm and breath deeply and slowly.
Cuddle a teddy.
Be glad to be with friends.
Be kind to everyone in your tent.

Children comment on their favourite night time school sleep over activities:

Since the school sleep over night I always look for the Plough now, every night, especially on my holidays.

There are sooooo many aeroplanes (or are they UFOs?)

Moonless night - no stars, but clouds. Now, that's when it feels REALLY dark..

I like to see Orion. I can spot the three stars on his belt, and the red star Betelgeuse too. I even taught my mum to find it.

The best thing ever is seeing a shooting star. We were in our sleeping bags just looking up. Everyone was so quiet. William fell asleep and had to be carried into his tent at the end, actually IN his sleeping bag by the teachers!

The glorious moon with craters visible- AWESOME!

I like to spot the satellites when they go over. You can tell them because of their very straight line. I wonder if they are looking at me looking at them!. Maybe they are spy satellites!

N is for night: learning stories

Going on a night walk: children's comments

Catching moon shadows is my favourite thing. The moon has to be just right for it. Bright is best. It's like there is magic everywhere. It works well when the ground is flat.

I felt nervous, but sort of relaxed too. Even though we walked in places I go to in the day time, it seemed so different and I was surprised how scary it could be.

I did notice that we walked closer together than usual on the night walk.

The tree silhouettes were quite spooky, but we knew they were just our usual school trees- and we're not scared of them in the day time… so why be at night? Hmmm…

'It was D-A-R-K in the trees. I'm used to street lights on. It feels so different at night.'

I just love it, out at night. Sometimes I go rabbiting with my Dad so I'm used to it.

Listening to night sounds

Nine year old Clare remembers a night concert at school camp.

We had to find a special leaf or stone and bring it for a night concert and that was our concert ticket. Mine was a leaf. I'd chosen it because it had round holes in it. Then we all sat in a circle and had to be really still and quiet. Our teacher said that the concert had begun and we had to listen for it to start. I remember hearing

Cars, like a background rumble some of the time.
Occasionally a roaring motor bike
Rustling nearby
Campfire crackles
Someone sneezing
Owls screeching, not hooting
Giggling from tents nearby, but the sound seemed very far away
*A very **loud** silence- how can that be?*

Afterwards I thought how did she know? How did she know when the concert would start? And I've thought about it a lot since too and now I think that really, there's ALWAYS a concert, but we don't listen to it. That's clever.
I've still got my leaf ticket.
I did my own concert for my family in the garden at home and it worked.

O is for *out and about*

WHAT MATTERS TO CHILDREN *being in different places, moving about in the world*

Big ideas:
- sorting
- classifying
- similarity and difference
- comparison
- habitats
- survival
- change
- growth
- decay
- life and death
- hypothesis
- evidence

'I believe that something that has grown from real things, real experiences has a great authority.'

Sir Anthony Gormley sculptor
The Guardian, 14.02.08. p27

INVESTIGATE

a range of **habitats**:
logs, ponds, puddle, a hole in a tree, under stones
ways in which **creatures** protect themselves from predators

plant variety: leaf shape, colour and surface; flower petal shape, colour and scent; seed dispersal mechanisms

owl pellets

Toolbox

binoculars   camera
coloured acetate sheets
compass   headtorch   magnifying glass
matchbox   plastic beaker
stethoscope   string
tape measure   torch
unbreakable mirror

USE the tools

Use the stethoscope to listen to tree sap rising; vibrations through a path or a wooden bridge; the sound of water falling and your heartbeat at the top of a hill.

Place a mirror on the bridge of your nose and look down at the reflection of the sky.

Find a place where the torch is really useful.

How many different things will fit in the matchbox?

How does looking through the blue colour acetate make you feel? How do greens change when seen through a red acetate? Which is your favourite colour world?

How big can you make a ladybird?

PHOTOGRAPH
a range of environments:
wet   dry   cold   shady   sunny   muddy
south facing   north facing

Questions worth asking
- Is all water rain?
- What trees have the best leaves for making an umbrella?
- What plants make green dye when boiled in water?

Children need access to a place where they can dig in the earth, build huts and dens with timber, take really great risks and learn to overcome them. They want a place where they can create and destroy, where they can build their own worlds, with their own skills, at their own time and in their own way.

Lady Allen of Hurtwood

DESIGN
kits to explore
- pond
- beach
- stream
- shadows
- an ancient wall
- meadow
- wind
- frost
- snow
- rain
- night
- trees

LIST
words that are particular to the place, such as…
- spray
- downy
- track
- glitter
- serrated
- linger
- humid
- trickle

IDENTIFY
five kinds of tree

Links with
First-hand experience: *what matters to children*   U is for under my feet
Learning: *what matters to children*   E is for learners learn everywhere

O is for *out and about*

Annabelle Dixon on seasonal challenges

Ice and snow present seasonal challenges to children's thinking. Even getting hold of the correct words isn't easy; I have heard children say 'frackerley', 'sneet' and 'owldrops' as variations on frost, sleet and hailstones. The whole experience of melting and freezing is deeply fascinating to young children but the interest is notably diminished if it is simply book-related, second-hand. We may 'know' the reasons for water suddenly going hard when reaching a certain temperature, but it is still an intriguing phenomenon. If we no longer respond with any great interest though, who and what was responsible for the shrivelling of our sense of wonder?

Movement, change, light, growth and decay are the lifeblood of nature… I need the shock of touch, the resistance of place, materials and weather, the earth as my source. I want to get under the surface. When I work with a leaf, rock, stick, it is not just the material itself, it is an opening into the processes of life within and around it.

Andy Goldsworthy, environmental artist

MAKE

a collection of plants stuck on a card backed with double sided sellotape

choose a theme for your collection for example, how many different greens can you find

use this as a starting point for a painting or coloured pencil drawing, extending from the edges of the card, matching colours, shapes, patterns and textures

---

Unique opportunities for children outside

collecting, hunting, tasting,
smelling, being alone,
being still, listening, exploring,
running and running and running
building, climbing, tracking,
watching change over time,
digging and burrowing, gardening

COLLECT

a feather

one seed with wings

a thorn

three shiny things

a very round stone

something fuzzy

something sharp

something pungent

something that makes a noise

something perfectly straight

something beautiful

a chewed leaf (not by you!)

something white

something soft

exactly ten of something

DRAW

five grasses or five leaves or five seed heads to show their differences

PAINT

two contrasting environments

DESIGN

a creature

make a habitat to ensure its survival

change the conditions- (climate, predators, environment) and

adapt the creature to cope with change

RECORD

a tree diary for a year

WRITE

labels describing your five favourite trees

Books for children

A Little Guide to Trees	Charlotte Voake
A Little Guide to Wildflowers	Charlotte Voake
Little Foxes	Michael Morpurgo
Ten Seeds	Ruth Brown
The Garden	Dyan Sheldon
Tree of Life: Charles Darwin	Peter Sis
We're Going on a Bear Hunt	Michael Rosen

Poems

Hiawatha	Henry Wadsworth Longfellow
Shades of Green	Anne Harvey

Books for adults

The Wild Places	Robert MacFarlane
Sharing the Joy of Nature	Joseph Cornell*
Hand to Earth	Andy Goldsworthy and Terry Friedman
Exercising Muscles and Minds	Marjorie Ouvry

*some ideas on this page can also be found in Joseph Cornell's work

 **is for** *pattern*

Big ideas:
repetition
reflection and rotation
sequence and symmetry
infinity

Patterns in storytelling

MAKE A STORY BOX
based on one of the following books:
James and the Rain Karla Kuskin
Rooster's off to see the world Eric Carle
Follow My Leader Emma Chichester Clarke
My Grandmother's Clock
Geraldine McCaughrean
and then...
Play the story
Tell the story
Make a simple book to record the story

Questions worth asking
What would life be like without pattern?

Books for children
Anno's Mysterious Multiplying Jar Masaichiro Anno
Getting to Know the Work of
Great Artists: Faith Ringgold Mike Venezia
MC Escher Kaleidocycles Doris Schattschneider
and Wallace Walker
Tar Beach Faith Ringgold
The Patchwork Quilt Valerie Flournoy
Poems
An Attempt at Free Verse Wendy Cope
Rhyme-Time Vernon Scannell
Books for adults
Islamic Designs Eva Wilson
The Encyclopedia of Quilting and Patchwork Techniques
Katharine Guerrier

INVESTIGATE *factorials*
READ 'Anno's Mysterious Multiplying Jar'
MAKE a factorial story of your own
The mathematical symbol of a factorial is an exclamation mark!
So the factorial of a number, followed by an exclamation mark, is the product of itself multiplied by all the whole numbers preceding it.
So 6! = 6x5x4x3x2x1= 720

INVESTIGATE Islamic Designs
Visit the local mosque to investigate three kinds of Islamic pattern:
Geometric (Vedic)
Calligraphic (script)
Arabesque (natural)

COLLECT *pattern words*
brindled, factorial, monotony, piebald, rhythm, tartan, tessellation, variegated, template, infinity

VISITS AND VISITORS
tile shops
formal gardens
a quilter
a florist
a butterfly farm

COLLECT *patterns in*
nature: broccoli, cauliflower, feathers, passion flower, pomegranate, shells, wasps' nest, butterfly and moth wings...
the made environment:
windows and doors, brick walls, roof tiles, thatching, solar panelling, wind farms, pargetting, beach huts, drain covers, fences, cobbles, paving slabs, chain links, tyre treads, soles of trainers and boots...
print:
wallpaper, wrapping paper, book covers and endpapers, chintzes...
horticulture:
ploughed fields, crops: food and forest, a vineyard, allotments, community gardens, hanging baskets...
discuss and select the most striking for a museum of pattern

FIND *pattern in the Artworks of*
Gustav Klimt, Paul Klee, Bridget Riley, Edouard Vuillard...

LISTEN TO *pattern in music*
The Goldberg Variations J.S. Bach
Bolero Maurice Ravel
Moonlight Sonata Ludwig van Beethoven

Links with
First-hand experience: *what matters to children* **V** is for variety
Learning: *what matters to children* **C** is for learners choose

PRINT patterns using potatoes, plasticine, card strips as printing blocks. Overlay one pattern on another.
STENCIL patterns using card cut-outs, sponges and paint.
MAKE a relief print block using card, string or Polystyrene Press Print. Use the block to print a pattern with reflected or rotational symmetry.
MAKE clay tiles with incised and applied motifs derived from your museum of pattern
DESIGN AND SEW a quilt with a group, for a special occasion

INVESTIGATE: The Vedic Square

The Vedic Square is a source of Islamic designs

Fill the cells of this number sequence with the multiplication of their row and column values
Reduce any value above 9 to its digital sum

e.g. 2x2=4
5x5=25 reduced to
2+5=7
9x9=81 reduced to
8+1=9

1	2	3	4	5	6	7	8	9
2	4							
3								
4								
5				7				
6								
7								
8								
9								9

Copy this several times
On one grid use a ruler to join all identical digits
e.g. all 2s. On another grid join all 3s, and so on

Or colour in identical digits
Look for connections/relationships between the shapes

1	2	3	4	5	6	7	8	9
2				1				
3								
4					1			
5	1							
6								
7			1					
8							1	
9								

1	2	3	4	5	6	7	8	9
2		8						
3								
4	8							
5						8		
6								
7					8			
8								
9								

Design a print block on Polystyrene Press Print or lino, based on
shapes from the Vedic Square
Use this to print a tile design
Compare this design with Islamic tile designs

Hold an exhibition of prints in your local mosque

INVESTIGATE: pattern in the man-made world

Scarlett age six

 **is for questions**

There is more to read about question - and answers - in chapter **Q** in *Learning: what matters to children.*

CHILDREN'S QUESTIONS

We have long been fascinated by children's questions and the evidence they provide of children's capacity for complex and innovative thinking. From our collections of children's questions, we have selected some examples that we hope show how listening to children's questions is always a rewarding and worthwhile activity. The examples fall into two very different categories:

CHILDREN'S QUESTIONS ABOUT RULES, ROUTINES AND PROCEDURES

Is mine better?
Can I go now?
Does it matter who wins?
Is it a curly 'c' or a kicky 'k'?
Where shall I start?
Please can I turn over?
Do I have to?
Who's going to look after us?
Can it be tomorrow?
If I wear tights, am I still a boy?

CHILDREN'S QUESTIONS ABOUT THE WORLD OUTSIDE THE CLASSROOM

Why is the moon broken today?
Why do fireworks go up?
Why don't plants grow in the moonlight?
Why can you see through glass when it's made of sand?
Would a polar bear melt in the desert?
What is love?
Can children make a bed?
Why are you pretty?
When I ask a question, where does it come from?

COMMENT

These questions illustrate children's concern both with doing things right and getting things right (related but not synonymous categories). The children also seem to be concerned with what lies behind the procedures, perhaps even expressing an anxiety that there isn't very much in the way of rhyme or reason behind the rules and regulations by which they are required to abide. One interpretation of these questions is that they are the questions of children who are learning to be dependent and obedient, at the expense of learning to be exploratory, adventurous free thinkers. As such they are useful feedback to educators who can learn, from questions like these, the extent to which their classroom rules make any kind of human sense to the children. But there are other, more rewarding questions that children ask.

COMMENT

These questions are, we believe, very different. They show children reaching out beyond the four walls of their setting into distant domains. In formal terms we can see the worlds of astronomy, physics, biology, psychology, philosophy and the huge world of emotional experience in which these children are already seasoned travellers. These children are exploratory, adventurous and free-thinking. They are learning about a wider and more intriguing world than the enclosed space of their benign classrooms. They are enthused by the world's mysteries and its contrasts. Any of these questions is not just worth listening to, it is worth taking seriously, exploring it and, of course, learning from it.

is for **questions**

Annabelle Dixon worked as a primary teacher for many years and always kept a question book. She writes:

How did I keep a question book?

I used to wear an apron with lots of pockets. People teased me about it, but I needed pockets for my little notebooks. In one of these, I recorded children's questions as and when they asked them. I just wrote them down. I didn't bother with questions like 'Where do the pencils go?' Or 'Are we going to assembly?' although of course, these may have told me something about particular children. I wrote down the children's questions that involved, for example, finding out, solving problems, reaching a conclusion or asking more questions. In the book area I kept a large 'Book of Questions' where I wrote down those the children asked to be recorded; we often used it at discussion times. I also noted down their comments about all the things they found out. I did it all the time, wherever we were.

Why did I keep a question book?

I first did this because of the influence that Piaget and both Susan and Nathan Isaacs had on my work with children. I wanted to push the edges of children's learning on as far as I could. In order to do this I needed to know what they wanted to learn. The questions they were asking became one of my tools for finding this out. I couldn't work without them as a guide, an aid to reflection and a vital source of feedback on the learning going on around me

Examples from the question book

'When did people first think of language?'

'When does the future start?'

'Do cats have to chase mice in real life?'

'How come little girls don't always do what their mummies ask?'

'Why do letters have names as well as sounds?'

What did I do with the questions?

Some questions were answered then and there, but others needed more of an exploration. I always asked children if they wanted their question to be shared with others. During the day I would feed back the ones I had permission to share. Children would offer suggestions and ideas. Some would team up to try and solve a problem and take the investigation further. Some preferred to work alone but they grew to value team work.

Children knew that their questions were taken seriously, but not always answered immediately. They came to understand that there were ways in which they could answer their own questions, and that they could share them with others. Our classroom culture was such that 'not knowing' and wanting to 'find out' were not only acceptable but could offer new excitements and insights. 'What if' and 'why' led them to view new experiences (or revisit old ones) at a level of real engagement, both emotional and intellectual.

The children's questions led the curriculum. As a professional, I knew the learning potential each one offered and I monitored what was done, and all the children's achievements.
The children's questions determined what resources they might need and what activities, visits and materials could best support them. The children had ideas for activities too, which I included in my planning.

 **is for questions**

An example from
Annabelle's
classroom

'Why aint water got no bones?'

Katherine had been pouring water from a teapot into a jug and back again for a full ten minutes.

Seeing the phenomena through Katherine's eyes was one thing; her imagery was so personal, so vivid. How to answer her question in any way that made sense was more than usually taxing. Eight years old and bound for a special education school the following term, it was the first observation of this kind that I'd heard her make.

Ellie answered for me.

" 'Course it's got bones! When it _freezes_, stupid! "

Katherine laughed. " Oh, yeah, " Silly me!

It was answer enough.

 **is for questions**

Questions worth asking and children's questions

Throughout the writing of this book we have been worrying about how to be helpful to educators without doing too much of their thinking for them. Too many helpful suggestions can be just as hard to handle as too few. The issue of questions is a particularly tricky one in this respect. We know from dozens of classroom studies that teachers ask an extraordinary number of questions: we don't need to encourage them to ask more. But we also know that many of these questions do not stimulate children's thinking or support their learning. Many questions simply ask children to remember, rather than explain, connect, pull it all together, imagine, invent new possibilities, compare, contrast, argue, reason… all the kinds of thinking we want children to do as they explore the world around them.

We have tried to solve this problem by including, on every page, a section called 'questions worth asking'. These are questions we hope will open up possibilities for exploring the topics we have selected: they are not the only questions that could be asked, but we hope they demonstrate how an unexpected question can lead to unexpected insights, unpredictable discoveries, and rich, meaningful learning. Questions stimulate quests to unknown territories and to far horizons. But by solving the problem in this way, we may have created another. We may unintentionally have suggested that the questions adults ask are more important and worthwhile than the questions children ask. On the contrary, we think children's questions are especially important starting points for the kinds of projects and enquiries we are advocating in this book.

Hypothesis or question – what is the difference?

Some of the educators who participated in the development of this book commented that some children make statements or formulate hypotheses, rather than ask questions. For example, one educator quoted a child who said: 'Everybody is symmetrical except dead people.' This is, grammatically speaking, a statement. But how simple (and how exciting) to take this statement, and reframe it as a question for other children to debate and discuss. Not just 'What do you think of Susan's idea?' but, 'Are people symmetrical? All people? Tall and short? Old and young? Living and dead?' and so on. It's well worth listening to children's talk for interesting and provocative ideas that could be turned into questions for worthwhile discussions.

As I type this page, a six year old child has just asked me, 'What do noses smell like?' Now we are both wondering...

 **is for** *questions*

The educator's responsibility for children's questions- what needs doing?

🌿 Listen to children's questions and write them down.

🌿 Respect and value children's questions - see them as genuine enquiries.

🌿 Make sure that all children have equal opportunities to ask questions.

🌿 Respond to children's questions in a variety of ways:

- with first-hand experiences (activities, visits, visitors) to take their learning on
- with discussion and debate, sharing their questions with others (children and adults)
- by helping them to make connections with other areas of their experience
- by using relevant story books.

Don't assume that it is the teacher's job to ask the questions and the children's task to answer them.

Remember, the more questions adults ask children, the less time there is for discussing children's questions, or for children to ask any.

Answering children's questions

Caroline Pratt (1867 – 1954) was a progressive educator who opened an experimental kindergarten in New York in 1914. In her old age, she wrote an enthralling account of her life's work, with the compelling title *I Learn from Children* (first published 1948). The following extract describes her approach to answering children's questions.

How much those five year olds taught me in two short months! …Basic and precious truths became clear. Secondhand knowledge was of little or no use to these children. Words are too recent an acquisition to a five-year-old: his tools of learning, the ones with which he is most capable, are still his own senses. When we thrust verbal information upon him, we are actually coming between him and the thing he is trying to learn. Devoted mothers who spend much of their time with their children in the early years should especially take this lesson to heart. Eager to give of themselves, they make the mistake of telling a young child too much, even in answering questions. Much later in my work I learned the truth of the discovery made by Lucy Sprague Mitchell [another progressive educator, whose husband was a close friend of John Dewey]: a young child's question is not always meant to be answered. It may be a way to open a conversation; it may be a question to which he himself wants to supply the answer, to verify a recently acquired bit of knowledge. That all children's questions must be answered is a rule with too many exceptions. A better rule is to let the child find the answer himself.

Pratt (1990:31-2)

Out of the questions of children shall we gradually come to discover what are the essentials of a perfect curriculum.

Ruth Griffiths (1939)

Books for educators

Dialogic Teaching	Robin Alexander
Dialogues with Children	Gareth Matthews
The Genius of Play	Sally Jenkinson
Well I Wonder	Sally Schweitzer

Q is for **questions**

Children's difficult questions

Why aren't you pretty?

Why doesn't praying work?

Why does Vasos keep making that noise?

Why did Fiona's brother get blown up?

Why does she smell funny?

Are soldiers good or bad?

Is she made of chocolate?

Why has Sarah got two mummies?

Why can't I call him 'Paki' when everyone else does?

Will there be a Tsunami on our beach?

Why is Johnny going to die next year?

Why am I here?

Why am I me?

Children sometimes ask questions that may seem personal, cheeky, philosophical, embarrassing, revealing, quirky or prejudiced – and certainly difficult to answer.

Some further suggestions for responding to children's difficult questions are given in *Action for Racial Equality in the Early Years: understanding the past, thinking about the present, planning for the future* by Jane Lane.

Educators need to be confident enough to be honest with children

This entails:

- being well informed about relevant political and cultural issues, both local and worldwide
- working as a staff group, anticipating questions and formulating sensitive responses
- critically examining personal values
- being clear about the values shared and agreed by the whole staff group.

Being helpful and truthful means:

- listening to these questions attentively, without making assumptions or judgements and without blaming or scolding the children
- sometimes saying that you don't know, but are prepared to find out or give it more thought
- supporting and encouraging children in thinking through the effect of their words and actions on others, seeing how words can hurt, and how the 'kindness of children' can prevail.

Children expect the help and truthfulness of grown-ups.

Loris Malaguzzi

The power (and limits) of reason

In arguing that it is important for children to think about the 'why' questions that most concern them, we do not want to suggest that every 'why' question can be answered with a completely satisfactory and reasonable answer. The power of reason is both enormous and limited.

Which of us can answer 'why' questions about earthquakes, avalanches or car accidents? Or say why some things move us to tears of joy? Or why we find some parts of our world incomparably beautiful? Some problems cannot be answered by the power of reason.

Children have the capacity to turn to the logic of the imagination, when the logic of the rational world doesn't seem to apply. In a review of Oscar Wilde's fairy tales for children, the author Jeanette Winterson puts it beautifully:

Reason and logic are tools for understanding the world. We need a means of understanding ourselves too. That is what imagination allows. When a child reads of a Nightingale who bleeds her song into a rose for love's sake, or of a Selfish Giant who puts a wall round life, or of a Fisherman who wants to be rid of his Soul … the child knows at once both the mystery and truth of such stories. We have all at some point in our lives been the overlooked idiot who finds a way to kill the dragon, win the treasure, marry the princess. As explanations of the world, fairy stories tell us what science and philosophy cannot and need not. There are different ways of knowing.

 **R** is for *rain*

WHAT MATTERS TO CHILDREN *how the world works, being in the world*

Big ideas:
extreme
solubility
protection
evaporation
water-*one of the four elements*
absorbent and repellent materials

VISIT
an umbrella shop
pumping station
reservoir
drains
gargoyles

go out in different
kinds of rain
visit the rain in
many different
places

LISTEN TO THE SOUNDS OF RAIN
under an umbrella
a tree   the hoods of
different rain coats…
inside a tent, a shed
a greenhouse
a conservatory
on a tin tray
a plastic sheet…

MAKE
rain   rain paint
bird baths   rain mud
gargoyles   rain music   a rain dance
things and surfaces to keep rain off
puddles (in mud, tarmac, shingle, sand)
rain go away   rain go down gutters
puddles disappear

Toolbox
big broom   guttering   hairdryers
metal, cloth and plastic buckets
mops   sponges   umbrellas
water butt   water hoover   water pump
water repellent materials
water wheel   wellies

INVESTIGATE
different ways of collecting rain
adding sand, paint, corn flour… to rain water
where rain can be found
objects which float on rain

protection from rain – homes, clothing
what rain feels, sounds and smells like
what happens when there is too much rain
(flooding) too little rain, and no rain (drought)
flood gates

animals when it's raining
worms in the rain and afterwards

how the world looks before it's rained
how the world looks after it's rained
how the world smells after it's rained
how the world looks when it's raining

rain clouds

puddle depths, shapes and sizes
the colour of rain
how to change rain water – freeze and heat

*…And rushing and flushing and brushing
and gushing...*   Robert Southey (1774-1843)

COLLECT
words about rain
drizzle   mist   monsoon   soak   steep
sea fret   gushing   pouring   splash
cats and dogs   drench   torrential...
pictures of the rain by
Hokusai   Hiroshige   Renoir   Rousseau

Questions worth asking
When is a cloud a rain cloud? How big is the biggest puddle?
Is a reservoir a puddle? When is a puddle a pond?
When is a puddle a flood? Why does rain come down?
What makes rain bounce? Does all rain bounce?
Is all mud rain mud? When does rain stop being rain?
Why does rain go sideways?
Does it rain on Mars? Is all rain the same?
Is there any water that is not rain? Where does the rain go (in the
place you live/at you school/ at the park/at a cathedral)? Is dog
spit rain? Who likes rain? What happens when there is no rain?
How wet can you get?(and how can you get dry again?)

*All children have the
right to enjoy the
essential and special
nature of
being
outdoors.*
Learning
Through
Landscapes

PLAY
MAKE a role play shop for rain
clothes or umbrellas
PLAY tennis in the rain, or petanque,
or hockey…

MUSIC
Pitter Patter Raindrops
use rain sticks make
your own rain sounds

Raindrop Prelude
Chopin

Singing in the Rain
*(and the video of the
dance too)*

Books for children
Alfie's Feet   Shirley Hughes
James and the Rain   Reg Cartwright
Puddleman   Roger Mc Gough
Rain   Manya Stojic
Rainy Day   Emma Haughton
The Water Hole   Graeme Base

Books for adults
City in the Rain   Reggio Children
From a Puddle   Reggio Children

Links with
First-hand experience: *what matters to children*   **W** is for water
Learning: *what matters to children* **U** is for learners thirst for understanding

R is for rain: a learning story

An exhibition of umbrellas

In a one-class entry infant school in a large industrial city, the teachers and children worked together to set up an exhibition of UMBRELLAS in the school hall, to entertain parents and families on the termly open evening. Every imaginable kind of umbrella was represented, from tiny cocktail stick umbrellas to a huge dark green angler's umbrella. The school photographer was persuaded to lend her silver umbrella; there were umbrella skeletons, parasols, bamboo umbrellas and many, many more. Children's observational drawings and clay models were added to the exhibition, together with documentation of the work of small discussion groups investigating the topic of umbrellas through talk. The following contributions shown here come from one such group, in a mixed class of five, six and seven year olds.

"They go up and down."

"Children's ones are smaller."

"They keep you dry – not all of you.

"You'd have to have a very big one to keep your feet dry."

"Babies have an umbrella on their pram – for the sun."

"Golf people have umbrellas."

"Without an umbrella your hair gets wet."

"Sometimes tables have umbrellas."

"Parasols are umbrellas."

"Umbrellas are made of plastic, cloth, metal, wood."

"People use them in the wet, not in the dry – except on the beach."

"Umbrellas have to have handles."

"An elephant doesn't use an umbrella – it's too big."

"Fishes don't use umbrellas."

"The umbrella for a monkey is a tree."

"A bus shelter is like an umbrella."

"Umbrella pines are a kind of tree."

"You can use an umbrella when you open a champagne bottle."

"Don't use one in the shower - you won't get clean."

"The roof is an umbrella to the house."

"The shell is an umbrella to the tortoise."

"Robots need them for the rust."

"A mushroom is an umbrella to a mouse."

"A rainbow is shaped like an umbrella."

"A hat or a jumper, or a newspaper, or a hood - all good umbrellas."

"The fleece is an umbrella for the sheep."

"A flower is an umbrella for the bee."

"A helmet is like an umbrella."

"Goggles are umbrellas for your eyes."

"A greenhouse is an umbrella for plants."

"Channel swimmers are covered in butter."

with acknowledgements to Bryony, Alan, Sarah, Hendrix, Helen, Alex, Katherine

 **S** *is for* surfaces

WHAT MATTERS TO CHILDREN *being in different places, making a mark on the world*

Big ideas:
cause and effect
safety
protection
transformation
form and function
friction
camouflage

VISITORS
an architect
a garden designer
a town planner
a stonemason
a theatrical make-up artist
a plasterer

TOUCH AND EXPLORE
wet sand   dry sand   gravel   stones
bark   moss   clay   paper   textiles
shingle   bodies   walls   tables   tyres

MAKE
an iced cake
a sand sculpture
a warning sign that is easily noticed

We are trying to make the best visual description our senses and our minds can achieve of a random sample of the reality that surrounds us. We want to see without motive and without reminiscence this cliff, this street, this roof, this field, this rock, this earth

Mark Boyle

Toolbox
palette knife   scarifier   sandpapers
graters   icing kit   files   chisels

INVESTIGATE
ways to add surfaces to things: icing a cake, tarmac, mulching a flower bed, pargetting a wall
wetting different surfaces
how many ways a surface can be changed
textured pictures which represent the earth's surfaces
movement across surfaces: wet sand, dry sand, tiles, long grass, short grass, concrete, asphalt, wood-block, carpet. Is it better to run, walk, crawl, slither? Design a sports arena to suit a variety of movements
ice/frost/snow: how is it formed? why is it slippery? how do ice skates work?
brakes: bicycle, car, wheelchair, pushchair. What makes a good brake?
tyres: racing bike, mountain bike, scooter, wheelbarrow, veteran car, lorry, bus, aeroplane, formula one
which tyres work best on gravel, mud, cycle path, grass and concrete? Why?
camouflage: colours that conceal, colours that attract attention
coverings: skin, feathers, hair, fur, fleece and scales, peel, crusts: how do they work?
waterproofing: rainwear, umbrellas, tents, roofs
carving: Greek and Roman friezes, the Rosetta Stone
surface tension: meniscus, thermometers, calibration, pond-skaters
reflection of light from surfaces: mirrors, periscopes, mirage
how to make smooth things rough and rough things smooth
soles of shoes
Braille

Questions worth asking
- How deep is a surface?
- Have clouds got a surface?
- Is a surface the same as a skin?
- Where does the surface of skin start and stop?
- Where does the surface of a round ball start and finish?
- Is there anything that has no surface?

WORDS
prickly   smooth
floppy   silky
uneven   gritted
hairy   fluffy
crinkled   sharp
hard   rutted   soft
squelch   solid
jagged...

INVESTIGATE
HOW TO MAKE engravings, etchings, wood cuts, lino prints and other relief prints using card, textured papers, clay, wire, wood, Polystyrene Press Print, string, sand, mud, natural materials, threads and fabrics, together with a range of mark-making tools to make a rich palette of resources
LOOK AT the engravings and woodcuts of Clifford Harper, Claire Leighton, Gwen Raverat, Robin Tanner, Thomas Bewick, Hiroshige, Hokusai
FIND OUT ABOUT the ice sculptures and sand sculptures of Andy Moss and Jamie Wardley

Books for children
Children's World Map — Collin's World Maps
Snail Trail — Ruth Brown
The Big Big Sea — Martin Waddell
The Earth From the Air for Children — Yann-Artus Bertrand & Robert Burleigh
The Wonderful World Book — Jennie Maizels & Kate Petty
Where the Forest Meets the Sea — Jeannie Baker

Books for adults
Double Harness — Robin Tanner

Links with
First-hand experience: *what matters to children*   **P** is for pattern
Learning: *what matters to children*   **E** is for learners learn everywhere

S *is for* **surfaces: learning stories**

MAKE
sand-casts using wet sand and plaster of Paris
rubbings of surfaces to use as a resource for a paper collage
collages of textured papers or fabrics
clay relief tiles
drawings of objects hidden in 'feely bags' (draw by touch alone)
wool windings to represent the texture and colour of natural objects such as shells, plants or stones
stitched surfaces to represent the texture and colour of surfaces, such as woodland, desert, the sun
weavings using a range of materials – threads, fabrics, plastic, grasses
paper landscapes using twisted, pleated, pierced, embossed and rolled papers
paintings using very thick paint or with additives such as glue, sand or sawdust
drawings on different surfaces – papers, walls, the pavement, chalk boards, perspex, glass
a 'feely tunnel' from cardboard boxes - line the interior surfaces with a range of materials to crawl through

Look at the surface of the Earth from the highest place you can

Grace age ten

Alphie age five

 # S is for surfaces: *learning stories*

The Fallen 9000

What is the Fallen?

Sand and ice sculptors Andy Moss and Jamie Wardley, from Sand In Your Eye, developed the idea of the Fallen Project (The Fallen 9000) together to mark Peace Day.

Jamie Wardley writes,
'The objective was to make a visual representation of 9000 people drawn in the sand which equates the number of Civilians, German Forces and Allies that died during the D-day landings, 6th June during WWII as an example of what happens in the absence of peace.

On the day we had 60-70 confirmed volunteers that had travelled from around the world to help. We knew that this was not enough to complete the project in the 4.5 hours that we had, so at 3pm when we were about to begin we were overwhelmed by the hundreds of people that turned up to help. Myself and Andy then began to explain the task ahead, and together did a demonstration on how to make a stencil in the sand. However, when we lifted the stencil I realized that we had just made together the first of the Fallen, a representation of a person that once lived; they had parents, family friends. This person had died prematurely due to a conflict and we were marking his passing.

When I make a sculpture or a drawing in my imagination that person is for a moment very much there, I will often find myself talking to them to see what they are thinking and how they are feeling, there becomes a connection between me and them. The person that we had drawn was very present indeed, we had made a connection and I was for a moment overwhelmed and Andy Moss had to continue.

is for surfaces: learning stories

After that hundreds of people took stencils and rakes in hand and embarked on drawing the 9000. The Peace Day project had finally begun in earnest represented by the people of the world. Of those people that were there were my mother, partner, and friends. This is poignant and when a person loses their life these are the people that are affected. What was profound were the people that turned up that I had never met. They believed in the same thing we believed in, a statement of Peace. Monika Kershaw was there remembering her son and his colleagues that died in Afghanistan and even wrote in their names beside them. George, a veteran who was on the D-Day beaches was also there and embraced the importance of the project as demonstrating the result of conflict. There was a group from Israel that drew together, people from Germany, Finland and as far as Chili.

During the day I was running up and down the cliffs taking photographs. What I found is that in this region there are many relics and monuments to the war but it is always difficult to visualize what the actual human loss was. On Peace Day we quietly and harmoniously drew 9000 people in the sand so that people can understand the loss with their own eyes. This was a quiet day with a very loud statement. The message of the Fallen is now travelling the globe, those people that lost their lives are no longer with us but on International Peace Day 21st September 2013 they spoke.'

 **is for thinking**

WHAT MATTERS TO CHILDREN *being in different places, moving about in the world*

Understanding the world

On these pages we summarise some of our own thoughts about children's thinking, the kinds of thinking that we value, the important kinds of thinking that are stimulated and fostered by first-hand experience.

Everyone has a favourite story to tell of a child who comes out with an apparently absurd comment on the world and its inhabitants: we tend to treat these fantastic, bizarre, even surreal remarks as charming, or laughable, or cute. In this book, our argument is that all children's thinking, however surreal it may seem, deserves to be taken seriously, as rational reflections on their experiences, and as considered contributions to their growing understanding. Loris Malaguzzi, one of the founding fathers of what we now think of as the Reggio Emilia approach, argues forcibly that the logic of children's thought straddles two dimensions: the logic of imagination as well as the logic of things. These two domains co-exist in a relationship of both turbulence and reciprocity, a relationship in keeping with the natures and desires of children. Indeed, he goes on to claim, their very identity emerges through the process of 'bringing closer together the frontiers of the real world, those of the possible and the impossible'. Vivian Gussin Paley, a supreme practitioner of the art of taking children's thinking seriously, makes the same point in a different way. She observes how the children in her kindergarten often solve puzzles and problems in the real world by recourse to fantasy and fairy tale. For Paley, this is not a weakness, but a sign of admirable elasticity of thought.
And, extending this thought, she explains:

As soon as (a child) learns a language well enough, and before he is told he cannot invent the world, he will explain everything.

This is thinking well worth taking seriously.

The five or six year old is ...not a captive of his illusions and fantasies, but can choose them for support or stimulation... He has become aware of the thinking required by the adult world, but is not yet committed to its burden of rigid consistency.　　　　　　*Wally's Stories*, p.81

From childhood we are on a special flight of wonder.

Albert Einstein

BOOKS FOR EDUCATORS

Children's Minds　　　　　　　　　　　　　　　　　　　　　　　　　　Margaret Donaldson
The Hundred Languages of Children - Advanced Reflections　　　Edwards. C, Gandini, L. and Forman G. eds.
Thinking Children　　　　　　　　　　　　　　　　　　　　　　　　　Anne Meade with Pam Cubey
Threads of Thinking: Young Children Learning and the Role of Early Education　Cathy Nutbrown

 **is for thinking**

TAKING THINKING SERIOUSLY

Annabelle Dixon's concept of 'tool words'
[An extract from a first-hand account of Annabelle's classroomfor five to seven year olds, drawing on observations made in 1996-7]

On the classroom notice board is a quotation from the philosopher Ludwig Wittgenstein (himself for a while an elementary school teacher, in the 1920s, in small village schools up in the mountains south of Vienna):

'The limits of my language are the limits of my mind.'

Annabelle's response to this warning is to structure much of her teaching around what she calls 'TOOL WORDS'. The first of these words to become important to her was 'problem', when she realised, some years ago, that without this word in their working vocabularies, children did not understand what was happening to them when they met a problem. She reasoned that if they could grasp what kind of an experience a problem was, they would more readily deploy their intellectual and emotional energies in finding ways of solving it. And so it proved. Once her pupils had grasped that a problem (a disagreement with a friend, a technical difficulty in a construction project, a puzzling observation of the natural world) could be relished, explored and finally resolved, they were much less likely to walk away from problems, to abandon their projects or to refer their disputes to adult authority.

Building on this discovery, and the children's appetite for more, Annabelle developed a list of essential TOOL WORDS for children's thinking [see the box alongside]. During one of my visits, Annabelle showed me the work the children had been doing on the school's behaviour policy document, which had recently been written in consultation with KS2 pupils. Annabelle's response to the policy was to ensure that the key words used in the document would be understood by the five, six and seven year olds in her class. She did this by building up definitions of words – such as 'respect' – drawn from the children's lives. Large sheets of paper recorded this work in progress:

'Keeping secrets from people isn't respectful.'
'Swearing at people isn't respectful.'

Annabelle overheard a child swearing quietly to himself one day, while searching in his tray for a missing treasure. When he saw her, he stopped, with a guilty flush, but not because his teacher had heard him.

'That's not respecting myself, is it?' he explained.

 **T** is for thinking

Children thinking with their hands

When children draw, paint, make a model, or a sculpture, or write a story or poem, their thinking becomes visible. We can see their response to experiences, real or imaginary. They show us what is important to them, what they have noticed and what they have felt. They use the tools and materials available to them to represent and express their thinking.

When children make their ideas visible in this way they think *with* the materials rather than *before* the materials are used. They plan as they make, adapting, changing, developing, enlarging, adding detail and definition to the work they are creating.

If we are to help children to express their thinking then the range and authenticity of the tools and materials are important, along with the knowledge of how they work. A range of mark making tools including iPads, card, paper, clay, wire, wood, sand, mud, natural materials gathered from the locality, threads and fabrics make a rich palette of resources. They are irresistible: children will use them to explore, investigate, classify, arrange, design, solve problems, imagine, observe and translate. Each representation will be personal and unique; the work of thoughtful hands.

At the Pablo Neruda School in Reggio Emilia, Italy, five and six year old children drew hands. Each drawing expressed delight and energy; the delight of confidence and the energy of purposeful action - this hand is waving, this one is kind, this one pointing the way. Afterwards the children reflected on their capacity to make drawings:

'Drawings don't just come from your hands, they come from your head too… because first you think and then you do the drawings with your hands.'

'It's fun to do the things you have in your mind. You do it with your hands and then the things you had in your head come out.'

'Ideas are in the brain, but they have to come out somewhere…. sometimes they come out of your mouth and sometimes they come out of your hand... hands have to think…'

five and six year old children from the 'Pablo Neruda' school, Reggio Emilia

Children thinking in their play

Children are expert thinkers. In play, they test out their ideas and theories; they recreate what they know of the world, from their own experiences. They work out 'what is' and 'what might be'. They experiment with materials and with other children to find out how things work and how things happen; they want to know how to make things happen for themselves. They explore alternative worlds of reality and fantasy and step into the shoes of others as they think as others might think. They behave as others might behave. They take themselves on journeys into other worlds, or their own familiar world: a hospital, a hairdresser's, a Traveller's trailer, living on a long boat, or finding Batman's cave, going to school at Hogwarts, being Dr. Who's assistant, or swimming in a mermaid lagoon. They check out rules of behaviour and social norms. They go on to invent and practise their own rules of behaviour and social norms. Children play with the things of the world and the people of the world, in different places of the world. They explore the important themes of love and hate, good and bad, powerful and weak, loss and loneliness. They try to make sense of world events and current affairs. In their play they think about, 'Who am I?' Who might I become?' 'What will that be like?' 'How can I keep safe in my world?' They magnificently wonder,
'What if….?' In their play children make sense of the world.

Play is a form of thought.

Piaget 1931

T is for thinking

'I don't know whether you have ever seen a map of a person's mind. Doctors sometimes draw maps of other parts of you…. but catch them trying to draw a map of a child's mind, which is not only confused, but keeps going round all the time. There are zigzag lines on it, just like your temperature on a card, and these are probably roads in the island; for the Neverland is always more or less an island with astonishing splashes of colour here and there, and coral reefs and rakish-looking craft in the offing and savages and lonely lairs and gnomes who are mostly tailors, and a cave through which a river runs, and princes with six elder brothers, and a hut fast going to decay, and one very small old lady with a hooked nose. It would be an easy map if that were all: but there are also the first day at school, 'religion', fathers, the round pond, needlework, murders, hangings, verbs that take the dative, chocolate pudding day, getting into braces, say ninety-nine, three-pence for pulling out your tooth yourself and so on: and either these are part of the island or they are another map showing through, and it is all rather confusing, especially as nothing will stand still.'

Peter and Wendy (J.M. Barrie 1911)

 **is for** *under my feet*

WHAT MATTERS TO CHILDREN *what is in the world, being in different kinds of places*

Big ideas: elements
time
change

COLLECT

specialist shoes

fossils from a quarry, a chalk pit,
a clunch pit,
cliffs, beaches, gravel driveways.
Were they animals or plants?
How can you tell?

stones from a variety of places.
sort them in a variety of ways and give
them names

MAKE A GEOLOGICAL MUSEUM

VISITORS

an education officer from
a landfill site

a gemologist

a geologist

*a marathon runner

*a mountaineer

*a potholer

*a rambler

*a rock climber

*remind them to bring their
specialist shoes

COLLECT sand, soil, clay, gravel, rock,
chalk, leaf mold, turf…
Use these to make a model of a
landscape.
Include hills, cliffs, rivers,
waterfalls, marshes, forests,
seashore, caves…
Where would you choose to live in this
landscape?

BUILD a settlement
What would happen if the climate changed?
What if…?

DAMN a stream on a beach and change the
course of the water

CREATE a small waterfall

MAKE boats from natural materials

DEVISE safe ways to cross a stream or a ditch

DESIGN AND CONSTRUCT a container to
collect rain water and use it to water your
garden

COLLECT wood for a fire

BUILD a fire and cook on it

BUILD a shelter

SLEEP outdoors – under canvas, under the stars

FOLLOW footpaths and map where you
have been

LAY A TRAIL using sticks and stones for
friends to follow. Provide them with a key to
the signs you use.

USE a compass on your way home to record
all the different directions you have taken.
Is it the same on the way back to school?

**Go
around
barefoot
for a
whole
day**

VISIT

an ancient track or drove   a bridle path

a cave or system of caves   a mining museum   an old railway track

a ploughed field   a quarry   a riverbank

a towpath beside a canal   a waterfall

people clearing drains, laying cable, digging foundations

places to look at tombstones

places to look at remains of Roman villas- mosaics and hypocausts

road works   tunnels, underpasses and underground railways…

MAKE sand sculptures, clay sculptures, chalk carvings

TAKE plaster casts of tracks in mud

USE different clays – red, buff, white, stoneware- to make
models of animals, landscapes, islands, cross sections of the
earth's crust…

Books for children

Fossil	Bill Thomson
Hidden Under the Ground	Peter Kent
My Map Book	Sara Finelli
Pebble in my Pocket	Meredith Cooper
Stone Girl, Bone Girl	Laurence Anholt
The Fossil Girl	Catherine Brighton
What`s Under the Bed?	Mick Manning and Brita Granström

Books for adults

The Old Ways: a journey on foot	Robert MacFarlane
Holes	Louis Sachar

Links with

First-hand experience: *what matters to children*   **W** is for water
Learning: *what matters to children*   **E** is for learners learn everywhere

is for *under my feet:* **learning stories**

Saving the planet from landfill

Several years ago, I visited the International Primary School in Brussels, where I was impressed by the nursery aged children engaged in sorting recyclable materials into the required categories and then dumping them into the appropriate recycle bins. This was a daily activity and very much entrenched in the ethos of the whole school and wider community.

What struck me at the time was how much more this authentic activity meant to children than sorting logiblocs, and they were doing it in several European languages! ...the next step was to move on to sorting for reusing, repurposing, or upcycling to ensure that nothing went to landfill sites.

Shoeless Bea: walking barefoot

After discovering that training for a half marathon hurt less afterwards, when running barefoot, Bea Marshall stopped wearing shoes altogether and has been shoeless for four years.
Writing about this experience in *The Guardian* newspaper (weekend magazine supplement, 15 February 2014) she describes how it feels,

Intense is the best way to describe the first time I walked barefoot outside. Every step sent new sensations through my feet and toes. It was exhilarating... It started to feel as if my feet were constantly being given an intense massage... I'd look forward to walking on different surfaces - I especially love the texture of the white paint on zebra crossings. Every street suddenly felt rich and alive... Every path and pavement is different and exciting. I go to the Peak District sometimes. The rocks there are the best, because you feel as if your feet are moulding round them.

...I think my feet will stay bare. It just feels right.

Intrigued by archaeology at first-hand

My year 4/5 class visited the Roman City of Verulamium. I had already made a pre-trip visit to plan out a day, which included a visit to the Roman wall, the mosaics and hypocaust, the museum and a walk around the park lake under which there is a Roman burial ground.

When we settled down for lunch, children were attracted by something that had not been there when I made my visit. There was an archaeological dig underway near the museum and the city cathedral. Children eagerly watched the archaeologists at work as they ate. Some went to talk to the workers about their project; they were searching for evidence of a monastery linked to the cathedral. The children quizzed them about techniques they were using for excavating, intrigued by their slow progress and patience.

After lunch we went into the museum and when we left to return to our coach I was told by the curator that he had never worked with such interested and engaged children. Of course, he might say that to every visiting teacher, but I was certain that seeing the dig site in action made a real impact on the children and their attitude to what was in the museum, especially, the skeletons in coffins, excavated near the museum, not far from the archaeologists they had seen at work.

The next week a group were keen to set up their own archaeological dig on the school field. So we did exactly that, giving the children a time limit until the end of term for their excavations, just like the St Albans archaeologists, who had been given a time limit by their sponsors.

 **V** is for *variety*

WHAT MATTERS TO CHILDREN *who is in the world, making collections*

 **Big ideas:**
diversity
uniqueness
community
similarity and difference

SOUNDS OF MUSIC
COMPOSE a piece of music to reflect an experience: a journey, weather, a place, a time of day, or an element such as water, air, fire
EXPLORE variety within each sound: volume, duration, pitch and timbre
variety within the range of ways of repeating the sound: speed and rhythm
variety within the overlaying of sounds, playing some at the same time: texture
LISTEN TO a Gamelan orchestra a brass band a jazz band/ a choir a quartet

COLLECT
envelopes, spoons, flags, calendars from different faiths/countries, the same story in different languages, different versions of the same story, creation myths

VISITS AND VISITORS
builders' yard   cheese stall   ironmongers
generations   joiner   farmers' market ..
zoos   farms   ponds   woods
litter of kittens

INVESTIGATE
an orchard   clouds   fingerprints
language   voices   lines   blue
papers   sounds   bells   spices
flavours   cooking pots

VOICES
speaking whistling singing humming shouting
grunting squeaking howling whispering growling
SOUNDS
blast, chime, clash, glissando, peel, ring, roll, scrape, tinkle, vibrate…

MOVEMENTS
creep, linger, crawl, amble, run, sprint, dawdle, slide, slither, step, lurch, dance, tip-toe, spin, jump, leap, spring…

INVESTIGATE
the same word in different languages
stamps from different countries
coins from different eras

MAKE a patchwork quilt
COOK different pasta shapes and eat them (or potatoes, rice, lentils, beans)
PLAN AND PERFORM a variety show
GROW, MIX AND EAT a salad
FIND AND DRAW the differences between four pine cones, oak leaves, big toes, spoons, lemons
PAINT a sky diary everyday for a month…
PLANT AND TEND a buddleia bush to attract a variety of butterflies
MAKE an annotated pressed flower/leaf collection
USE a variety of cooking pots
PHOTOGRAPH people in action, hands, animal expressions, yellow...
MAKE a pattern of sounds using percussion instruments. Record the music in such a way that it can be played again.

Questions worth asking
- Can you have the same again?
- Are two of anything exactly the same?
- If you cannot make blue, red or yellow, how is it that there are so many different blues, reds and yellows?
- Why do people listen to the same music again and again?
- Why do people listen to many versions of the same song?
- How can you tell identical twins apart?
- Is there a place with no variety?

COMPARE drain covers pillar boxes lamp posts…

VISITS AND VISITORS
zoos
rock pools
aquarium
botanic garden
places of worship
seashore
ponds
woods
Balinese Gamelan
orchestra
symphony orchestra
choir
litter of kittens

Books for children
A Four-Tongued Alphabet   Ruth Brown
Goldilocks Variations   Allan Ahlberg
Honestly, Red Riding Hood was Rotten!
The Story of Little Red Riding Hood as Told by the Wolf   Trisha Speed
The Creation Story   Norman Messenger
The Fire Children: a West African Folk Tale Eric Maddern and Frané Lessac
The Further Adventures of the Owl and the Pussy-Cat   Julia Donaldson
Tree of Life   Peter Sis
What Mr Darwin Saw   Mick Manning and Brita Granström
Poems
Classic Poetry an illustrated collection   Michael Rosen
The Cat and the Fiddle, a treasury of nursery rhymes   Jackie Morris
Pied Beauty   Gerard Manley Hopkins
Books for adults
An Experiment in Education   Sybil Marshall
White Teacher   Vivian Gussin Paley

Links with
First-hand experience: *what matters to children* **C** is for colourful curriculum
Learning: *what matters to children* **B** is for learners belong to a community of learners

V is for variety: a learning story

A variety of artists

A newly amalgamated junior, infant and nursery school held an art exhibition to celebrate their coming together and the opening of a new building, the Link, built to connect the formerly separate schools.

The children made their art to reflect their understanding of links, connections and their changed relationship with each other. They identified buildings and things that function as links – buttons, chains, pins, bridges, hands – and used these as springboards for making a variety of art.
The nursery children made clay tiles impressed with leaves collected from trees around the school. The tiles had holes in the corners so each could be connected by string to make a hanging.

Four and five year olds, having explored the properties of buttons, used them to inspire designs for prints and photograms.

A visiting environmental artist, Jane Thewlis, worked with six year old children to make beautiful sculptures using leaves pinned together with pine needles. When hung on frames against the windows, the light filtered through, making a connection between the world indoors and the world outside.

The seven year olds made a collage of photographs of places around the school that had special significance for them. The collage itself became a new starting point for observational drawings on paper and then on acetate sheets that were overlaid on the collage. This created an extraordinary illusion of three dimensions.

In the two parallel classes of eight year olds the children made weavings to reflect the colours and textures of the local environment and pastel drawings of chains. These were vibrant; using only the three primary colours each link made a secondary colour at the point of contact.

The nine year old children used screen printing to show a range of bridge designs – suspension, cantilever, swing, single and multi-span arches – linking places separated by water, rail and road.

Ten year olds explored the paper cut outs of Henri Matisse. Using digital aided art they showed how each cut out shape could be moved and placed in a new relationship to other shapes to create a range of variations on the original work of art.

The oldest children in the school, aged eleven, focused on the centrepiece of the Sistine Chapel, where Michelangelo shows God reaching out to Adam at the moment of creation. They studied hands; the ways in which they express feelings by touching, stroking, holding, rubbing, shaking and slapping. The drawings were large, expressive and beautiful.

For a short while the school became an art gallery; the children showed each other, their parents and visitors around, sharing and celebrating their achievements.

From one central theme grew a rich variety of expression.

What had the children learned?

They had developed an understanding of the concepts of linking, joining and connecting. They had learned a variety of techniques to express their understanding and had developed skill in using these.
Most importantly for this school at this time the children had learned to respect and value each other as they grew together as one community.

 **W** *is for* **WATER**

WHAT MATTERS TO CHILDREN   *what is in the world, understanding how the world works*

 **Big ideas:**
water - one of the
four elements
diversity
cause and effect
similarity and
difference
no water, no life

COLLECT
colours of water
paintings of water *(the sea paintings by
Emil Nolde, Canaletto, Turner,
Ivan Hitchins, Maggie Hambling
Nicola Bailey's illustration in
The Mousehole Cat…)*
smells of water
sounds of water (and record them)
things that won't work without water

USE
a canvas bucket
a metal bucket
a clothes line
a salad spinner
a whisk
cloths, sponges
brushes and rollers
containers for carrying water
gutters, fall pipes, tubing and hose pipes
funnels
siphons and pumps
pipettes
soaps
water timers
wheelbarrows
absorbent materials

INVESTIGATE
crossing water without getting wet
how water feels how water moves
how water changes
pond skaters moving on water
ways water changes things
the shape of water   ways water can travel
where water pipes go how people use water
your water footprint

MAKE
a dam   a pond
a whirlpool
an aqueduct
ice   mud
paintings wet on wet
things disappear in
water
water disappear

EXPERIMENT WITH
pepperpot
flour sifter
sieves
watering can
sprinkler
turkey baster

VISIT
a car/bus/train wash
a pumping station   a hydro electric dam
an aquarium
bridges over water   canals   locks and weirs
duck ponds   fords   fountains
hairdressers/barbers
swimming pools   puddles
launderettes   lighthouses
waterfalls   working water wheels

COLLECT water words
torrent splutter drizzle
gush spatter mist
liquid vapour swirl
meniscus…

LISTEN TO
The Aquarium
Saint-Saens
Vltava Smetana

Questions worth asking
Can you wash water?
If mud is made of earth and water, why
do people call it dirty?
Where do tears come from?
How wet can you get?
Which is worse; no water or too much
water?
Whose water have we used when we
eat imported food?
How old is water?

*If there is magic in
this planet, it is
contained in water.*
Loran Eisley

WASH
a baby
a dog
a floor
a jumper
a window
a wall
a potato

FIND
the smallest bit of water   the largest bit of water
a place to play pooh sticks   a spring   a well
an underground stream   different ways of containing water

Books for children
Come Away From the Water Shirley   John Burningham
Little Whale's Song   Fran Evans
Little Grey Men   BB
The Storm   Kathy Henderson
The Water Babies   Charles Kingsley
Water Dance   Thomas Locker
Wet World   Norma Simon
The Snowflake, Winter's Secret Beauty   Kenneth Libbrecht
and Patricia Rasmussen

Poems
Out and About   Shirley Hughes
Paper Boats   Rabindranath Tagore
The Cataract of Lodore   Robert Southey
The Brook   Alfred Lord Tennyson

Links with
First-hand experience: *what matters to children*   O is for out and about
Learning: *what matters to children* O is for obedience and desire in learning

Finding out about water

Watching young children explore the nature of water makes you realise how much there is to know about it. That it can vanish into thin air as steam, acquire solidity as ice, and then as snow become as separate and soft as downy feathers: these are just a few aspects of coming to know the ways of this strange runny stuff. Because of all its fascinating variations, water is an element that lends itself to 'finding out' like none other. Not just what it does when it rushes up tubes and down funnels, not just how you try to catch some in your hand or squeeze it into bottles that won't take any more, but also what water does to things. Children may know the wetness of rain and baths and, if they're lucky, the wetness of puddles and streams. What they may not know about, for instance, is the wetness of cardboard once it's been immersed. And what happens to clay, paint, flour, sugar?

Dissolving or vanishing?

After a class discussion about 'dissolving', a colleague filled four large jars with water; at her invitation, the children added sand to one, flour to another, sugar and salt to the last two. The children (5-7 year olds) shook them, stirred them and watched what happened. About ten minutes into the investigation, a worried looking six year old approached his teacher.
'I'm afraid I've lost the salt. It's gone.'

The flour hadn't gone, nor had the sand; someone else was stirring the sugar. He was encouraged to taste the water and acknowledged it was salty, but it seemed he still had great misgivings. If there was any doubt about where he was in his thinking, it was dispelled by what he did next. What could happen to salt (magic?) might happen to sand: stirring it with a teaspoon didn't seem to work. Undeterred, he and a friend searched for bigger and bigger spoons, as it seemed to them that size of spoon might be the clue to the problem. They finally found a spoon so large it wouldn't go into the jar. That was it! They were convinced that had they been able to squeeze it into the jar, the sand would have vanished.

Does water always run down hill?

What too, of siphons, water wheels, pumps, sprays and taps? Another colleague and her class followed an interest in these aspects of water for a whole term. It wasn't exactly what she'd planned but the degree of motivation was extraordinarily high as they followed up questions posed by themselves after each new investigation. Their enquiries included writing to a manufacturer of water toys, visiting a working water-mill and going to the local swimming baths. They were still trying to find out if it was true that water always ran downhill when the term ended. They had looked at weirs, dams, and drains. They had considered the making of islands and the falling of rain. Thoughtful, generous provision was made as the children's interests moved from one question to the next.

Whose question is it?

A colleague of mine was once asked by a child 'What shape is water?' This question led to the most intriguing and imaginative experiences for her class. Different shaped containers were filled with coloured water and poured from one to another. It was frozen into different shapes and boiled off into clouds of condensation. It was poured onto the playground and the flow and puddles were closely examined.

The children's questions kept the level of involvement very high. Pleased with what had happened, my colleague then posed the same question to another class. This time there was little more than a polite flicker of interest. As she herself recognised rather ruefully, the question had not belonged to the children and their interests at that moment. She could have persisted through the force of authority, but he recognised that without motivation, the value of the subsequent learning would have been minimal.

The extracts on pages 91 and 92 come from the writings of Annabelle Dixon

 **is for water:** *learning stories*

Finding out – the teacher's dilemma

Stacey and Vicky asked for large, housepainter brushes. They took them and a large bucket of water outside onto the playground.

Stacey: *'Look, we've found out something! We paint the wall [bricks] and by the time we get to the other end, it's disappeared!'*

Vicky: *'I remember doing this in the nursery, but I don't remember it doing this!'*

They both agreed it was a hot day and that the sun is shining on the brick wall, but, after no little consideration, decide this is not a factor in the disappearance of the water 'paint'.

'Why not?' I ask. I'm genuinely interested to know.

'The water has been sucked into the bricks,' is their answer.

Of course, most of their experience has been of absorption. Evaporation is a new idea.

I was about to ask why they thought their mothers hung out washing, particularly on sunny days. Then I remembered that they didn't. You don't if you live in a block of flats and you run the risk of having your washing pinched, if you hang it out in the communal area on the ground floor. It's easy to take children's experience for granted.

Maybe it's something they could do themselves - choose some clothes that need washing from the dressing-up corner. I thought that maybe they could make and draw round puddles, especially on surfaces they'd already found out were waterproof, like plastic sheeting.

That's not to say they'll find out or generalise anything about evaporation. They may become fascinated by the way water rolls around on plastic, or where puddles stop; they may wonder why clothes are heavier when sodden. They may want to find out how big can a drip get before it stops being a drip, or how many dry clothes fit into the washing up bowl compared to the number of wet ones.

I'll know more when they tell me what they've 'found out'. And even more revealing will be when they tell me what's most surprising to them about what they've found out.

As it happens, they return to 'painting' the bricks, with much discussion going on between them.

They're still puzzled, so I decide that maybe it is an appropriate moment to suggest that it might be something called 'evaporation'. I explain a little about it and ask them if this seems to fit their experience?

They have some further discussion between themselves and then Vicky is the spokesperson:

'We've thought about that new word, that evaporation and we don't think it is that, do we Stacey?'

Why not save the children all their bother and take them out of their confusion, by simply telling them?

I could indeed, and there may well be times when I think it's the most appropriate thing to do. But the teacher's decision has to be based on what's most or least effective in furthering children's understanding. If the explanation, the 'telling', is close to the children's own first-hand experience, then it probably will be effective.

That's a very good question. One that most people don't bother to ask…. I bet you're always asking tricky and interesting questions like that. And you're not happy until you get a decent answer, right? That's good. That means you're already thinking like a scientist. Now you just need to find out more – and to keep on asking questions about all the new things you discover..

Glenn Murphy (2011)

W is for **water**: *learning stories*

Educators getting wet

Although our first edition already has an alphabet section *'R is for rain'*, we decided to add this section, *'W is for water'* to emphasise the opportunities water offers as a first-hand experience.

The *'W is for water'* alphabet page has been trialled with many educators from 2006-2012 across the England as a workshop session on courses led by the What Matters to Children team. It started as an *'R is for Rain'* workshop, but as we couldn't guarantee delivering a practical workshop on rain, if it wasn't raining on the conference day, this section was developed for non-rainy days.

Reflecting on some of the workshops with educators, I cannot fail to remember those who took part as involved, active, engaged, resourceful, determined, questioning and often laughing. Sometimes the water activities took place out in the community, sometimes they were on play areas, school grounds, or natural places where water is found, and sometimes indoors too. Conferences took place in different places- on site in settings, where we were grateful to be able to utilise the resources to hand, as well as add some of our own: a few took place in smart hotels, where we loaded pipes, guttering, hoses, water carriers, plastic sheeting, buckets, pond-wader-leggings and all manner of equipment referred to in the boxes on the earlier *'W is for water'* page.

In Cornwall, one headteacher investigated 'where water pipes go' and followed pipes in her nursery. Talking this through with staff, they discussed the merits of installing a completely transparent wash basin and clear pipe work right up to the to the drain- if such a thing was on the market. She even mentioned having a toilet with a transparent flush system so that children could see the path of water.
In Worcester, children were taken on visits to a nearby stream at different times of the year.

Many educators spoke of to their commitment to extending the variety and scope of water activities, so that children had a much more generous water environment, with more time for their explorations. Some became committed to taking children to water art installations in their local community and to places where water is found in the natural environment.

Over to you...

Role playing with water

In their play, five year olds set up an ice-cream store using ice-cream tubs full of water for strawberry, chocolate and vanilla ice-cream. They served these to customers using real ice-cream scoops and insisted on dipping their scoops into another tub of water between each serving.

Inside, having recently been visited by one of the local hairdressers, children played at hairdressers for themselves, washing hair tenderly and precisely as they had learned from their visitor. They used the play props of a chair, boxes for basins and rubber shower sprays for washing and rinsing. They used imaginary water on each other, but real water on their dolls and toys. None of the children were keen to have a real hair wash.

 **X** *is for* experts

---

A definition of learning

A teacher studying for an Advanced Diploma was given a 'homework' task to carry out in her classroom: finding out how children define the term 'learning'. She set to work the very next morning, and, notebook in hand, approached the nearest child in the room with the challenging question: 'What is learning?' And the five year old child answered proudly 'Learning is what I do.'

A little history

'In 1910,' writes Lifton, 'Warsaw society learned, with some surprise, that Janusz Korczak intended to give up a successful medical practice and literary career to become the director of an orphanage for Jewish children. Few people understood that medicine alone was no longer enough for this visionary paediatrician. The orphanage would give him a chance to put some of his educational ideas into practice.'

He remained at the orphanage until 1942, when he and all the orphans were sent to the death camp at Treblinka. But the fame of his progressive practice did not die with him. One commentator describes the orphanage in these words: 'a democracy of children, wherein children had a voice in governance, had duties and responsibilities, monitored their own work and progress, participated in daily routines, organised their recreation, and developed social consciousness by peer co-operation and supervision ... the children were the prime movers and doers of life in the orphanage. The adults there [Korczak and his few assistants] all came under its regulations ... There was a children's court, a parliament, a court of peers, a children's newsletter, and a committee of guardians ... It decreed that all children should have the right to be loved, the right to be listened to, the right to respect, the right to a past and a present as well as a future.'

In chapter K of our second book, *Learning: What Matters to Children,* we discuss the proposition that children know more than adults think they do. On this page/pages, we take the argument further, and suggest that children have much to tell us about their learning, that they are, indeed, experts on the subject. To support this proposition, we give a brief account of the great Polish-Jewish champion of children, Janusz Korczak (1878 – 1942). We draw on Korczak's own writings and the inspiring biography by Betty Jean Lifton, *The King of Children.*

When I am Little Again (1926)

This is the title of a marvellous book in which Korczak develops his big ideas. It is a tender fantasy, written in the first person singular, in the voice of a child. Some extracts will illustrate his right to be called 'the king of children'.

There seem to be two kinds of life: theirs – serious, worthy of respect, and ours – as if a joke. Because we're smaller and weaker, it's like a game. And this is the source of neglect. Children – these are future people. And so it's a matter of their becoming, it's as if they don't exist yet. But indeed, we are; we live, we feel, we suffer. Our childhood years – these really are the years of life.

They think that we easily forget, that we don't know how to be grateful. But it's they who forget. We remember very well. A year, even longer. Every rudeness and injustice, every remark, every one of their good deeds. And we can forgive a lot too, if we notice any kindness and sincerity.

If the grownups only asked us, we'd advise them correctly ... We know better what bothers us; we have more time to think about and observe ourselves; we know ourselves better; we're together more often ...

We are experts of our own lives and affairs.

 **X** is for *experts*

Big and little

In a short publication, *The Child's Right to Respect* (1929), Korczak identifies a damaging flaw in our thinking about children; in his own words: 'we learn very early in life that big is more important than little.' He goes on: 'Respect and admiration go to what is big, what takes up more room. Small stands for common and uninteresting. Little people mean little wants, little joys, little sorrows. A big city, high mountains, a tall tree – these are impressive. We say: 'A big deed, a great man.' A child is small and doesn't weigh much. There is less of him too. We must bend down, reach down to him. Even worse, the child is weak.'

Korczak's vision:

'We will build a school where children will not be learning dead letters from a lifeless page; where, rather, they will learn how people live, why they live, how they can live differently, what they need to learn and do in order to live full of the free spirit.'

Experts in Room 13

In 1994, a group of children in Caol Primary School in Fort William, Scotland, set up an art studio in an empty room: Room 13. They elected a management team and a managing director, opened their own bank account and ran the studio as a business. They employed an Artist in Residence, bought in equipment and supplies, staged exhibitions, took on commissions, sold photographs, stationery and artworks to generate a profit and occasionally applied for grants to fund their ongoing activities. From the original primary school in Scotland, Room 13 has grown into an international network of student-run arts studios, serving an expanding community of young artists in schools.

Do you remember?

Danielle Souness, aged 11, Managing Director of Room 13, Caol Primary School, Fort William, speaking to a Creative Partnerships conference at Dartington Hall, November 2003:
'Do you remember what it was like to be 11 or 12? Think!
You knew what was going on, you knew about war and sex, you didn't believe in Santa or the Tooth Fairy. You could think for yourself. You occasionally got things wrong because you couldn't understand something – but even adults do that.
Can you remember what it was like for adults to treat you as if you were something slightly different from a human being?
It was horrible, wasn't it? It still is.'

Books for adults

King Matt the First   Janusz Korczak

Questions worth asking

- Does Korczak exaggerate?
  'A teacher eagerly adopts the adult's privilege: to keep an eye on the child, not on oneself, to register the child's faults, not one's own.'

- Can this be true?

The last word

In the very last lines of *The Child's Right to Respect*, Korczak calls for humility, as well as respect, in the presence of childhood, and closes his argument with an unforgettable tribute to children: 'It is precisely the children who are the princes of feeling, the poets and thinkers'.

 **Y** *is for* yesterday

WHAT MATTERS TO CHILDREN *exploring the world, finding out how the world works*

Big ideas:
change and unchangeableness
chronology
justice
memory
similarity and difference
style
time

MAKE *a story box*

Make a story box for a true story - this may be a story told by a grandparent/uncle/friend. The story box will have enough things in it to help re-tell the story to someone else.

FINDING OUT ABOUT YESTERDAY

LOOK AT paintings-
What can we learn about time past?
Haymaking Pieter Breughel (1565)
The Doctor Sir Luke Fildes (1887)
The Foundling restored to its Mother Emma Brownlow (1858)

READ stories about memory, the past or with pictures set in the past

MAKE a role play area of an archaeological camp and decide what tools you need
What can you find out from broken and incomplete objects?

FIND a place where you can dig to find remnants of the past

LOOK AT 'then and now' photos and spot the differences and likenesses

VISITS AND VISITORS

people with stories to tell about their memories
museums – dinosaurs, transport, armour, costume, childhood
living history museums
old places – houses, churches, castles, ruins, caves…
burial places
monuments and memorials

MEMORY

What is memory?
READ *Wilfrid Gordon McDonald Partridge* by Mem Fox.

MAKE a memory box for yourself.
What will you put in it to help you remember?
What are souvenirs? Do you have any?
How do you remember:
your last birthday?
a day out?
a holiday?
your granddad?

LOOK AT THINGS MADE IN THE PAST

Authentic things to handle
Things to use
Things to provoke enquiry
Things to story with
Have you seen anything like this before?
What do you think it could be?
What questions would you like to ask about it?

MAKE A TIME CAPSULE FOR TODAY

What will you put in it? –
DVD?
app.?
photos of yourself, your family, your home?
newspaper?
video recording?
Where will you keep it?
When will you open it?

Imagination is remembering with a special kind of intensity. Jill Pirrie

Questions worth asking
- What is yesterday?
- When was yesterday's yesterday?
- How many yesterdays are there?
- What does old look like?
- What is time?
- Am I standing on the edge of yesterday or the edge of tomorrow?

PLAY
Kim's Game and Pairs to practise remembering

Books for children

Do Knights Take Naps?	Kathy Tucker
Little Stowaway	Theresa Tomlinson
Mockingbird	Allan Ahlberg and Paul Howard
My Grandmother's Clock	Geraldine McCraughrean
The Best Christmas Present in the World	Michael Morpurgo
The Diary of a Young Girl	Anne Frank
The Garden	Dyan Sheldon
The Granddad Tree	Trish Cooke
The Velveteen Rabbit	Margery Williams
When Grandma Came	Jill Paton Walsh
Wilfrid Gordon MacDonald Partridge	Mem Fox

Books for adults

A Little History of the World	E.H. Gombrich
The Bucket: memories of an inattentive childhood	Allan Ahlberg
The Young Ardizzone: an autobiographical fragment	Edward Ardizzone
Learning from Objects	Gail Durbin, Susan Morris and Sue Wilkinson

Links with
First-hand experience: *what matters to children*   C is for collections
Learning: *what matters to children*   X is for learners expect the help and truthfulness of grown ups

Y is for yesterday: learning stories

Family history

Working in a mixed age class with children from four to six, the Yesterday project fitted nicely into the theme on family history, which was part of the school's rolling plan. It offered many opportunities for numeracy (sequencing events, using vocabulary to describe time) and literacy (re-telling stories, making books, stories with similar settings, recognising question marks and question words). In my weekly planning, which I share with my teaching assistant and pin on the board for parents to look at. I put a list of 'questions worth asking', mostly taken from the sheet. Using the sheet helped me to keep focused on the idea of 'what matters to children?'

Timeline activity

I asked the children to draw a picture of 'something that happened a long time ago', and then we arranged the pictures in order of time. There was a wide variety in their responses: some drew the same picture they always draw (my birthday, my family, my holiday): many thought quite deeply about 'something that happened a very long time ago'. Some children were confused about when their chosen event happened: were they two, three, four? - while others were very precise: 'My birthday party was at the same time that Fatima was on holiday.' The older children were pleasantly competitive about who could get the first entry: Billy really thought he'd won with 'When Great Aunt Molly was a little girl. Because, she's the oldest person in our family.' He was very crestfallen when Adam came up with, 'Life before man'.

Our yesterday timeline

I recorded what children said about their pictures, and they positioned them on a timeline. We left a very large space at the end for 'tomorrow'.

This is when nobody is alive on earth or water, not even an ant or a shark.

Lizards a long time ago before there were people.

When Great-Aunt Molly was a little girl. She's the oldest person in our family.

When my mum was a baby Nanna and Poppa looked after her.

When my mum was little a big boy threw a stone at her. She was a schoolgirl.

My mum and dad got married.

My mum and dad got married in New Zealand.

When I was in my mummy's tummy.

After I popped out of my mum's tummy.

When I was a baby I was in a cot.

I was a baby.

I sat on my sister's lap when I was zero.

I was a baby when Oliver and Charles were little boys.

When I was a baby Billy was only little.

A long time ago my uncle came to see me when I was a baby.

When I was a baby I went to the beach on a rainy day.

It's raining and I'm on the beach holding an ice cream. I was one year old.

When it was Christmas my brother and sister woke me up. I was two.

I went fishing and I didn't catch any fish. I was three.

When it was my fourth birthday.

My old school before I came to this school. It was called Britannia Village. My dad worked there.

I went fishing with my grandpa and my dad a long time ago when I lived in Utah, last summer. I caught a whale with a grown-up hook.

It was my birthday. I went on holiday last week.

I am going to school today

...TOMORROW

 **is for yesterday: learning stories**

The story box project

I asked all the children to bring in a story from home, from the childhood of one of their parents (or about themselves when they were small). If they wished they could bring in a box and props to help them tell the story. The parents were very excited about it, and many of them put a lot of work into making a box with their children. Two of the children knew what story they would tell from the first moment I introduced the project: Mario knew he would tell us about fishing in his father's childhood village in Italy, and Harry had a story from his mother's schooldays.

To begin with a group of children told me their stories from memory and I scribed them onto the computer and printed them out in book form for them to illustrate. We read these to the rest of the class. Every time the children retold the stories they used the same words and phrases. When the stories were printed out they found them easy to read. Some of the children have started to make their own books in the class 'office' – usually more complex than the ones I showed them how to make, using masses of paper and sellotape.

Fatima's story
My mummy lived in Uzbekistan. She lived there. I was born in Uzbekistan. My grandma has a big house. It has a round box with toys in it.

Mario's story
When I was little I went to Messina with my dad. I went fishing at night. I saw a dolphin on the way to the place where I was going to fish. I saw a helicopter landing on a volcano. I caught lots of fish. I caught three at a time sometimes. When I got home I ate the fish.

Harry's story
When my mum was a little girl she was at her school. A big boy threw a stone at her. She got a big lump on her forehead. You can still feel that lump on her head now.

Adam's story
My great grandma told me a story. A long time ago she owned a shop. It was a fruit shop. It was called Tom Heydon. When granddad was a little boy he helped in the shop.

Other 'golden moments' of learning about yesterday came in activities that are old favourites.

We played a variation of the game 'My grandmother's cat' called 'My teacher's teddy': the children passed round an old teddy bear of mine, adding an adjective each time:

'My teacher's bear is an old, patched, ripped, dusty, one-eyed, broken bear'.

The next day Thomas and Phoebe brought their newer teddies in to compare. Bobby said,

'I can tell they're not old because they're not all those words we said about your bear.'

'I have a large cake-tin full of sherds. Personal archaeology; garden archaeology, from the two old houses in which I have lived… There were tantalising finds. A tiny green glass bottle, just over an inch high. Nineteenth century by the look of it. But what could it have held? And a little, delicate, cream-coloured horn spoon, another valued item, surely lost rather than discarded. This was not archaeology, of course. It was fortuitous discovery…It is not enough to live here and now… The past is irretrievable but it lurks. It sends out tantalising messages, coded signals in the form of a clay pipe stem, a smashed wine bottle…I can't begin to understand what that time was like, or how the men who made them lived, but I can know that it all happened… To have all those sherds in the cake tin expands my concept of time.'

Penelope Lively

Y is for yesterday: learning stories

The allure of strange things from yesterday

An education adviser, Ruth, brought an object to a workshop exploring the big ideas children meet when they handle a strange and puzzling object. It was metal, made in Sheffield, and had a handle attached to a hollow cuboid container measuring three and a half inches by two by one the depth of which could be altered by raising and lowering a plate. The educators were baffled. For what possible purpose had this been made? They worked out the mechanics of the tool but were mystified by its use. Could it have been used for pressing or printing? If so, what, how?

The story was told to a delighted audience. This object had been brought to Wales from Russia by Ruth's great-grandmother, Florence. Born in 1880 in a Welsh village, Florence went to live in Odessa as a child, but with unrest and revolution the family returned to Wales. While growing up in Russia she had learned to make ice-cream and brought this skill home with her.

Ruth writes, 'My father, (Florence's grandson, born in 1926) remembers her little wooden ice-cream shop across the road from her house. Great-grandma used milk from the family farm and eggs. Ice was sent up from Newport, the nearest town. Using a wooden tub and two paddles the mixture was turned and turned. As a small boy it was my father's job to turn the paddles; his treat was licking them at the end. The ice-cream was served sandwiched between wafers and sold for a farthing, a ha'penny or a penny depending on the depth of the scoop. In between customers, the scoop was dipped in water'.

That's what it was, an ice-cream scoop with an adjustable base! The educators handled it again. You wouldn't have got much ice-cream for a farthing! How intriguing. What a lovely thing.

What had the educators learned?

They had listened to and learned from a family story, valuing the past and its connection to the present. They had wondered at the skill of past technology, and delighted in handling a well-crafted object. They had experienced the process of enquiry from investigation and hypothesis to understanding. All from one object.

Yesterday in children's art

Brothers and sister Oliver, Annabel, and William (aged 12, 10, and 9) wanted to do something vibrant and bright to remind their mother of the amazing, once-in-a-lifetime, ski holiday they had been on together earlier that year. At their community children's art club, they painted acrylic pictures for her to give as presents at Christmas.

They proudly announce that they each spent 22 hours on their individual works of art, planning their pictures, looking at holiday photos, talking about their experiences. As they set about constructing their pieces and painting, the young artists recalled happy holiday memories.

The final pictures show the general snow scene, aspects of the resort- runs, chalets, chair lifts, life on the slopes, the splendour of the mountains and the heavily snow laden trees, which they painted while often quoting the Wordsworth poem they had learned on the holiday, 'Every branch big with it, bent every twig with it'.

On each painting there is a self portrait showing an accurate record of the ski outfits they wore and depicting a specific memory of the skiing- Oliver's spectacular wipe out, Annabel's stylish parallel skiing, William's overall joy and constant smile.

The pictures hang in the hall of their house; when the family look at them, or explain their artworks to visitors, they not only remember memories of their skiing, but also, the hours they spent on them; the pre-planning and replanning, their style of painting and the techniques they used, as well as how they worked well together and really enjoyed it. Of course, they do not fail to mention the unforgettable expression on their mother's face when she opened them on Christmas day, and neither does she.

| Annabel age 10 | Oliver age 12 | William age 9 |

 **Z** is for **zigzag**... *finding your way through the book*

This is the final letter of the alphabet and so we take this opportunity to re-emphasise the big ideas about children's learning that run through the whole book.

PROVIDE

Active learners need nourishing food...
...so educators provide a rich curriculum diet:
living animals and plants, natural materials, intriguing and useful artefacts, interesting people of all ages, big ideas, puzzling ideas, contrasts and consequences, identity and differences.

THE NOUNS OF LEARNING

ORGANISE

Children are active learners...
...so educators organise opportunities for them to:
act on the world, touch and taste it, explore it, ask questions, compare and contrast, listen and look, collect bits of it, discuss and debate all the interesting things they meet.

THE VERBS OF LEARNING

VALUE

Educators value children's learning...
...but children's learning is not to be weighed and measured with de-contextualised assessment tools. It is better understood as an exploration, a journey, a narrative.

LEARNING STORIES

We are drawn to the metaphors of journey and narrative as ways of understanding children's learning, but we do not believe that journeys must always follow the same route, or that there is only one ending to a story or only one way to tell it.

The structure of this book invites educators to devise routes and create learning stories of their own invention, following their children's threads of interest in the world around them – a world of shifting seasons and sensations, unpredictable happenings and exhilarating surprises.

The suggestions in this book are not to be followed in strict alphabetical order: we hope educators will discover zigzag routes of their own, as their children make new connections and build new bridges between different aspects of their learning, Doors to Keys for example, in earlier pages.

The Big ideas: section on each page may be a helpful way of identifying an interesting next step to take – but there is no substitute for paying close attention to children's spontaneous talk, play, drawings and other representations, to see which way the grain of their thinking lies. This kind of attention, listening and looking respectfully, is the key to the educator's responsibility to work 'with the grain', in Annabelle Dixon's memorable phrase, rather than teaching 'across the grain'.

is for zigzag... *finding your way through the book*

WORKING FROM PRINCIPLES

Since 2005, and the first edition of this book, the What Matters to Children team have worked to define and refine a set of principles that have formed the basis of their conferences, presentations and workshops. Because of their growing importance in our thinking we have chosen to lay them out in the closing pages of this new edition. We are, in a sense, showing our hand, making explicit the basis for every line that we have written.
And here they are:

- The principle that first-hand experience is a necessary and significant element in children's learning.

- The principle that children are active learners who think and feel for themselves, and who use their hands, eyes, ears and their whole bodies to explore the world.

- The principle that children are powerful learners who learn from each other as well as from everything and everyone in the world around them.

- The principle of WHAT MATTERS TO CHILDREN – the four domains of children's learning - that ensures emotional involvement and intellectual engagement.

- The principle of adult involvement in learning: that educators can provide for, organise for and value children's learning.

- The principle that educators are people who can think for themselves, individually and together, making choices that will ensure worthwhile learning.

- The principle that children and adults can work together to build a harmonious learning community, with shared memories, principles and priorities.

These are the principles that need thinking about whenever educators exercise their power to make wise choices in the interests of children's learning. They are designed to provoke questions, to stimulate discussion and debate about how to make good use of them. The principles represent the big ideas that will support educators in their central responsibility: making a difference to the quality of children's learning. This paramount responsibility – to think for oneself and to make wise choices – was memorably emphasised by Robin Alexander in the *Cambridge Primary Review*, (2010: 308)

Pupils will not learn to think for themselves, if their teachers are expected to do as they are told.

being in the world

A is for
alphabets
& apples

B is for
bags &
brushes

C is for
collections &
colourful
curriculum

D is for
doors

E is for
enemies

F is for
furniture

G is for
goats, goldfish,
guinea pigs
& other
gorgeous
animals

H is for
homes

**acting on
the world**

Z is for
zigzag
through
the book

Y is for
yesterday

X is for
expert

W is for
water

V is for
variety

over
to
you ...

I is for
I
the active
learner

J is for
joining

K is for
knowing

L is for
looking
&
listening

M is for
mixing

**exploring
the world**

U is for
under
my feet

T is for
thinking

S is for
surfaces

R is for
rain

Q is for
questions

P is for
pattern

O is for
out &
about

N is for
night sky
&
night time

**thinking
about the
world**

People who buy

First-hand experience: what matters to children
by **Diane Rich, Mary Jane Drummond and Cathy Myer**

also buy

Learning: what matters to children
by **Diane Rich, Mary Jane Drummond and Cathy Myer**

Order copies from Rich Learning Opportunities

www.richlearningopportunities.co.uk

office@richlearningopportunities.co.uk

References

Adams, S., Alexander, E., Drummond, M.J. and Moyles, J. (2004) *Inside the Foundation Stage: Recreating the Reception Year* London: Association of Teachers and Lecturers

Adventures in Art (1997*) Adventures in Art: the Yellow Cow Sees the World in Blue* London: Prestel

Ahlberg, A. (2012) *Goldilocks Variations* Somerville MA: Candlewick Press

Ahlberg, A. (2013) *The Bucket: memories of an inattentive childhood* London: Viking

Ahlberg, A. and Howard, P. (1999) *Mockingbird* London: Walker Books Ltd.

Ahlberg, A. and J. (2003) *Peepo!* London: Viking Books

Ahlberg, J and A. (1999) *Cops and Robbers* London: Penguin

Alexander, R. (2008) *Towards Dialogic Teaching: Rethinking Classroom Talk* York: Dialogos

Alexander, R. (Ed) (2010) *Children, their World, their Education. Final Report and Recommendations of the Cambridge Primary Review* London: Routledge

Allen of Hurtwood, Lady (1968) *Planning for Play* London: Thames and Hudson

Allen, J. (1993) *Who's at the Door?* New York: Tambourine

Anholt, L. (2006) *Stone Girl, Bone Girl* London: Frances Lincoln

Anning, A. and Ring, K. (2004) *Making Sense of Children's Drawings* Maidenhead: Open University Press

Anno, M. and Anno, M. (1999) A*nno's Mysterious Multiplying Jar* London: Penguin Putnam Books

Ardizzone, E. (2010) *The Young Ardizzone: an autobiographical fragment* London: Slightly Foxed

Armitage, D. and R. (1994) T*he Lighthouse Keeper's Lunch* London: Scholastic Hippo

Armstrong, M. (2010) *What Children Know: essays on children's literacy and visual art* Lulu.com

Bailey, L.H. (1922) *The Apple Tree* New York: MacMillan Company

Bailey, L.H. and Jack, Z.M. (2008) *Liberty Hyde Bailey: essential agrarian and environmental writings* New York: Cornell University Press

Baker, J. (1989) *Where the Forest Meets the Sea* London: Walker Books

Bancroft, B. (2004) *An Australian ABC of Animals* Surrey Hills: Little Hare

Barber, A. (1990) *The Mousehole Cat* London: Walker Books Ltd.

Barnes, R. (1987) *Teaching Art to Young Children 4-9* London: Allen and Unwin

Barrie, J.M. (2004) *Peter and Wendy 100th anniversary edition* Dorking: Templar Hodder and Stoughton (first published 1911)

Base, G. (2004) *The Water Hole* London: Puffin

Baum, L.F. (2008) *The Wizard of Oz* London: Puffin (first published 1937)

'BB' (2012) *Little Grey Me*n Oxford: Oxford University Press

Bender, R. (1994) *A Most Unusual Lunch* New York: Dial Books

Bertrand, Y-A. and Burleigh, R. (2002) *The Earth From the Air for Children* London: Thames and Hudson

Bertrand, Y-A. and Burleigh, R. (2002) *The Earth From the Ai*r London: Thames and Hudson

Bettelheim, B. (1950) *Love is Not Enough* Glencoe, Ill: Free Press

Blake, Q. (2001) *Tell Me a Picture* London: National Gallery Company Ltd.

Blake, Q. (2012) *Quentin Blake's ABC* London: Red Fox

Blizzard, G.S. (1992) *Animals in Art* (Come Look with Me) Charlottesville, VA: Thomasson-Grant

Board of Education (1933) *Report of the Consultative Committee on Infant and Nursery Schools* London: HMSO (The Hadow Report)

Bolliger, M. (1976) *The Giant's Feas*t Reading, MA: Addison-Wesley

Borges, J.L. (2013) *A Course in English Literature* New York: New Directions p104

Bowler, T. (2012) *Blade: Enemies* Oxford: Oxford University Press

Boyle Family (1986) *Beyond Image (Catalogue for the Boyle Family Exhibit)* London: Arts Council of Great Britain

Brett, J. (1993) *The Mitten* London: Hodder Wayland

Brighton, C. (2000) *Fossil Girl* London: Frances Lincoln Ltd.

Brown, C. and Nassher, A. (2013) *Secrets of the Apple Tree* Lewes: Ivy Press

Brown, M.P. (2010) *The Lindisfarne Gospels and the Early Medieval World* London: The British Library

Brown, R. (1992) *A Four-Tongued Alphabe*t Red London: Red Fox

Brown, R. (2000) *Snail Trail* London: Andersen Press

Brown, R. (2010) *Ten Seeds* London: Andersen Press

Browne, A. (2008) *Hansel and Gretel* London: Walker Books

Browne, E. (1995) *Handa's Surprise* London: Walker Books Ltd.

Burnford, S. (2013) *The Incredible Journey* London: Vintage

Burningham, J. (2000) *Come Away from the Water, Shirley* London: Red Fox

Burningham, J. (2004) *The Magic Bed* London: Random House Children's Books

Canfield Fisher, D. (1913) *A Montessori Mother* London: Constable

Canfield Fisher, D. (1999) *The Homemaker* London: Persephone Press (first published in 1924 by Harcourt Brace Jovanovich)

Carle, E. (1998) *Little Cloud* London: Puffin

Carle, E. (1998) *The Mixed up Chameleon* London: Puffin

Carle, E. (1999) *Roosters Off to See the World* New York: Aladdin Picture Books

Carndele, J.M. and Vivas, P. *Park Guell: Gaudi's Utopia* (English version) Barcelona: Triangle Postals

Carr, M. (2001) *Assessment in Early Childhood Settings: Learning Stories* London: Paul Chapman

Cartwright, R. (1995) *James and the Rain* New York: Simon and Schuster

Central Advisory Council for Education (1967) *Children and their Primary Schools* London: HMSO (The Plowden Report)

Charles, P. (2008) *M is for Moose* Canada: Cormorant

Chevalier, T. (2013) *The Last Runaway* London: Harper Collins

Chichester Clark, E. (2001) *Follow My Leader* London: Harper Collins

Clarke, A. and Moss, P. (2001) *Listening to Young Children: the Mosaic Approach* London: The Joseph Rowntree Foundation (National Children's Bureau)

Clarke, M.C. (2002) *Ndbele* London: Thames and Hudson

Clarke, P. (2007) *Spotters Guide to 100 Things to Spot in the Night Sky* London: Usborne

Cole, B. (2001) *Drop Dead* London: Red Fox

Collins (2010) *Children's World Map* London: Collin's Maps

Cooke, T. (2000) *The Granddad Tree* London: Walker Books Ltd.

Cooper, M. (1996) *Pebble in my Pocket* London: Frances Lincoln

Cooper, S. (2003) *Frog* London: Random House Children's Books

Cornell, J. (1998) *Sharing Nature with Children* 20th anniversary edition Nevada City CA: Dawn Publications

Cousins, J. (2003) *Listening to Four Year Olds* London: National Early Years Network

Cox, B. and Cohen, A. (2011) *The Wonders of the Universe* London: Collins

Cox, P. (2001) *An Abstract Alphabet* San Francisco: Chronicle Books

Darling, J. (1994) Child-Centred Education and its critics London: Paul Chapman

Darwin, C. (1859) *On the Origin of Species* London: John Murray

de Paola, T. (1990) *The Indian Paintbrush* London: Hutchinson

de Rosay, T. (2008) *Sarah's Key* London: John Murray

de Waal, E. (2011) *The Hare With Amber Eyes* London: Vintage

Department of Education and Science (1990) *Starting with Quality: The Report of Inquiry into the Quality of the Educational Experiences Offered to 3 and 4 Year Olds* London: HMSO (The Rumbold Report)

di Lodovico Buonarroti Simoni, M. (1551) *Creation of Adam* Fresco. Rome: Sistine Chapel

Dinglo, A. and Basher, S. (2007) *The Periodic Table: elements with style* London: Kingfisher

Donaldson, J. (2002) *Room on the Broom* London: Macmillan Children's Books

Donaldson, M. (1987) *Children's Minds* London: Fontana Press

Doran, E. (2004) *A is for Artist* London: Tate

Drummond, A. (1992) T*he Willow Pattern Story* New York: North South Books

Drummond, M. J. (2011) *Assessing Children's Learning* (Classic Edition) London: David Fulton (first published 1993)

Duckett, R. and Drummond, M.J. (2009) *Adventuring in Early Childhood Education* Newcastle upon Tyne: Sightlines Initiative

Durbin, G., Morris, S. and Wilkinson, S. (1990) *Learning from Objects* London: English Heritage

Edwards, C., Gandini, L. and Forman, G. (2011) *The Hundred Languages of Children* Norwood N.J.: Ablex

Edwards, C., Gandini, L. and Forman, G. eds. (1998) *The Hundred Languages of Children: advanced reflections* Greenwich: Ablex (second edition)

Einstein, A. (1959) in *Albert Einstein, Philosopher, Scientist* Schlipp, P. A., (ed) New York: Harper Torchbooks

Einstein, A. (1973) in Bernstein, J. R. *Einstein* London: Collins

Euphan Todd, B. (2008) *Miss Ranskill Comes Home* London: Persephone Press

Evans, F. (2003) *The Little Whale's Song* London: Piccadilly Press

Fearnley, J. (2003) *Billy Tibbles Moves Out!* London: Harper Collins

Fearnley-Whittingstall, H. (2012) *Three Good Things* London: Bloomsbury

Fermor, P.L. (2013) *A Time For Gifts* London: John Murray

Feynman, R. (1968) *What is Science?* in The Physics Teacher 7.6. 313-20

Finelli, S. (2007) *My Map Book* London: Walker Books

Flournoy, V. (1985) *The Patchwork Quilt* New York: Dial Books

Fox, M. (1984) *Wilfrid Gordon McDonald Partridge* New York: Kane/Miller

Frank, A. (2007) *The Diary of a Young Girl* London: Puffin Modern Classics

Fraser, G. and Gestwicki, C. (2002) *Authentic Childhood: Exploring Reggio Emilia in the Classroom* Albany, NY: Delmar Thomson Learning

Garfield, S. (2011) *Just my type: a book about fonts* New York: Penguin

Geraghty, P. (2003) *Over the Steamy Swamp* London: Red Fox

Goldsworthy, A. and Friedman, T.C. (2006) *Hand to Earth* London: Thames and Hudson

Gombrich, E.H. (2005) *A Little History of the World* London: Yale University Press

Gonsalves, R. (2003) *Imagine a Night* New York: Atheneum Press

Gormley, A. (2014) *The Guardian* newspaper 14.02.08

Graham, K. (2013) *The Wind in the Willows* Oxford: Oxford University Press Ware (first published 1908)

Graham, M. in National Advisory Council on Creative and Cultural Education (1999) *All Our Futures: Creativity, Culture and Education* London: DES (The Robinson Report)

Gravett, E. (2007) *Orange Pear Apple Bear* London: Macmillan Children's Books

Gravett, E. (2010) *The Rabbit Problem* London: Simon and Schuster

Griffiths, R. (1930) A Study of Imagination in Early Childhood London: Routledge and Kegan Paul

Guerrier, K. (2001) *The Encyclopaedia of Quilting and Patchwork Techniques* Tunbridge Wells: Search Press

Guinness World Records London: Guinness World Records

Haddon, M (2004) T*he Curious Incident of the Dog in the Night-time* London: Vintage

Haddon, M (2008) *The Sea of Tranquillity* London: Harper Collins

Hanson, P. (2003) *My Granny's Purse* New York: Workman Publishing

Hart, S. Dixon, A. Drummond, M.J. and McIntyre, D. (2004) *Learning without Limits* Maidenhead: Open University Press

Haughton, E. (2000) *Rainy Day* London: Transworld Publishers

Hawking, L. and S. (2008) *George's Secret Key to the Universe* London: Random House

Henderson, K. (1992) *In the Middle of the Night* London: Walker Books

Henderson, K. (1997) *The Little Boat* London: Walker Books

Henderson, S. (2000) *The Storm* London: Walker Books

Hines, B. (2000) *A Kestrel for a Knave* London: Penguin Classics

Hodgkin, R. (1985) *Playing and Exploring* London: Methuen

Hoffman, M. (2001) *The Colour of Home* London: Frances Lincoln Ltd.

Holmes, E. in Holmes, G. (1952) *The Idiot Teacher* London: Faber and Faber (reissued by Spokesman, 1977)

Holt, J. (1990) *How Children Fail* (revised edition) London: Penguin

Hooper, M. and Kitchen , B. (1988) *Tom Crean's Rabbit* London: Frances Lincoln

Hughes, S. (2004) *Alfie's Feet* London: Red Fox

Hutchins, P. (2002) *Don't Forget the Bacon* London: Random House Children's Books

Huxley, A. (1962) *Island* London: Chatto and Windus (reissued by Flamingo, 1994)

Isaacs, S. (1929) *The Nursery Years* London: Routledge

Isaacs, S. (1930) *Intellectual Growth in Young Children* London: Routledge and Kegan Paul

Isaacs, S. (1932) *The Children We Teach* London: University of London Press

Jeffers, O. (2005) *How to Catch a Star* London: Harper Collins

Jeffers, O. (2006) *Lost and Found* London: Harper Collins

Jenkinson, S. (2001) *The Genius of Play* Stroud: Hawthorn Press

Jensen, V. A. (1977) *Sara and the Door* Reading, MA: Addison-Wesley

Katzen, M. and Henderson, A. (2004) *Pretend Soup and Other Real Recipes* Berkley CA: Tricycle Press

Kerr, J. (2008) *When Hitler Stole Pink Rabbit* London: Harper Collins Children's Books

Kingsley, C. (2003) *The Water Babies* London: Award Publications

Kolbe, U. (2007) *Rapunzel's Supermarket* Sydney: Peppinot Press

Koralek, J. (1994) *The Boy and the Cloth of Dreams* Cambridge, MA: Candlewick Press

Korczak, J. (1992) *When I am Little Again* and *The Child's Right to Respect* Maryland: University Press of America (First published in Polish in 1926 and 1929 respectively)

Korczak, J. (2005) *King Matt the First* London: Vintage (first published in Polish in 1922)

Kuskin, K. (1996) *James and the Rain* London: Hodder Children's Books

LaFleur, S. (2012) *Eight Keys* New York: Random House Children's Books

Lambert, S and S.A. (1997) *Best of Friends* London: Frances Lincoln Ltd.

Lane, J. (2005) *Action for Racial Equality in the Early Years: understanding the past, thinking about the present, planning for the future* London: National Children's Bureau

Learning and Teaching Scotland (2000) *The Structure and Balance of the Curriculum: 5-14 National Guidelines* Dundee: Learning and Teaching Scotland

Learning Through Landscapes (2004) Vision and Values Statement www.ltl.org.uk

Levi, P. (2000) *The Periodic Table* London: Penguin

Lewis, C.S. (1998) *The Lion the Witch and the Wardrobe*, illustrated by Christian Birmingham, Godalming: The Book People Ltd

Libbrecht, K. and Rasmussen P. (2003) *The Snowflake, Winter's Secret Beauty* Stillwater MN: Voyageur Press

Lifton, B. J. (1989) *The King of Children* London: Pan Books

Lindbergh, R. (1993) *Johnny Appleseed Boston* MA: Megan Tingley Books

Lionni, L. (2011) *Frederick* London: Anderson Press

Lipton, H. and Morgan, D. *The Adventures of Odysseus* Cambridge MA: Barefoot Books

Little, K. and Vilga, V. (2009) *The Blackest Hole in Space* London: Hodder Children's Books

Lively, P. (2013) *Ammonites and Leaping Fish: a life in time* London: Penguin Fig Tree

Lobel, A. (1994) *The Great Blueness* New York: Harper Collins

Lobel, A. (2004) *Frog and Toad Make a List* in The Frog and Toad Collection. New York: Harper Trophy

Locker, T. (2003) *Water Dance* New York: Harcourt Children's Books

Lum, K. and Johnson, A. (1998) *What!* London: Bloomsbury

MacDonald, G. (1982) *Castle Warlock* London: Samson Low

MacFarlane, R. (2007) *The Wild Places* London: Granta Books

MacFarlane, R. (2013) *The Old Ways: a Journey on Foot* London: Penguin Books

Maddern, E. and Lessac, F. (2006) *The Fire Children: a West African Folk Tale* London: Frances Lincoln

Madonna (2009) *Mr Peabody's Apples* London: Puffin

Mandela, N. (2004) *The Long Walk to Freedom* London: Abacus

Manning, M and Granstrom, B. (2004) *What's Under the Bed?* London: Franklin Watts

Manning, M. and Granström, B. (2009) *What Mr Darwin Saw* London: Frances Lincoln

Marshall, S. (1963) *An Experiment in Education* Cambridge: Cambridge University Press

Matthews, G. (1984) *Dialogues with Children* Cambridge, Mass: Harvard University Press

McAfee, A. (1998) *Why do the Stars Come out at Night?* London: Random House Children's Books

McCarthy, C. W. (2011) *The M.C. Escher Pop-Ups* London: Thames and Hudson Ltd.

McCaughrean, G. (2003) *My Grandmother's Clock* London: Harper Collins

McGough, R. (2007) *Puddleman* London: Red Fox

McLerran, A. (2004) *Roxaboxen* London: Harper Trophy

Meade A. and Cubey, P. (2008) *Thinking Children: Learning about Schemas* Maidenhead: Open University Press Melvin, A. (2007) An A to Z Treasure Hunt London: Tate Publishing

Messenger, N. (2001) *The Creation Story* London: Dorling Kindersley

Micklethwait. L. (1994*) I Spy Animals in Art* London: Picture Lions

Micklethwait. L. (1996) *I Spy Transport in Art* London: Picture Lions

Mitton, E. and Pal, E. (2010) *I See the Moon* London: Frances Lincoln

Mitton, J. and Ballit, C. (1998) *Zoo in the Sky* London: Frances Lincoln

Mobility of Expression Scuole et Nidi d'infanzia Reggio Emilia, Italy, 1995 - December 2003, (7th printing)

Moomaw, S. (2013) *Teaching STEM in the Early Years: Activities for Integrating Science, Technology, Engineering, and Mathematics* St. Paul MN: Redleaf Press

Moore, I. (2004) *Six Dinner Sid* London: Hodder Children's Books

Morpurgo, M. (2011) *Friend or Foe*   London: Edgmont UK Ltd.

Morpurgo, M. (2011) *War Horse* London: Edgmont UK Ltd.

Morpurgo, M. (2013) *Little Foxes* London: Edgmont UK Ltd.

Morpurgo, M. (2013) *The Best Christmas Present in the World* London: Egmont UK Ltd.

Morris, W. (1880) quotation from *The Beauty of Life* a lecture before the Birmingham Society of Arts and School of Design

Moss, A. (2013) *The Fallen 9000* www.sandinyoureye.co.uk

Munro, R. (2004) *Doors* Zurich: North-South Books

Munsch, R. N. (2003) *The Paper Bag Princess* London: Scholastic Press

Murphy, G. (2011) *Black Holes and Stuff* Macmillan Children's Books

Nicholl, H. and Pienkowski, J. (2004) *Meg and Mog* London:Puffin

Nickl, P. (1990) *Crocodile, Crocodile* Zurich: North-South Books

Nix, G. (2003) *The Keys to the Kingdom: Mister Monday* London: Harper Collins

Nix, G. (2004) *The Keys to the Kingdom: Grim Tuesday* London: Harper Collins

Nix, G. (2005) *The Keys to the Kingdom: Drowned Wednesday* London: Harper Collins

Nix, G. (2006) *The Keys to the Kingdom: Sir Thursday* London: Harper Collins

Nix, G. (2007) *The Keys to the Kingdom: Lady Friday* London: Harper Collins

Nix, G. (2008) *The Keys to the Kingdom: Superior Saturday* London: Harper Collins

Nix, G. (2010) The Keys to the Kingdom: Lord Sunday London: Harper Collins

Noddings, N. (2003) *Happiness and Education* Cambridge: Cambridge University Press

Norton, M. (2011) *The Borrowers* London: Puffin (first published 1955)

Nutbrown, C. (1999) *Threads of Thinking: Young Children Learning and the Role of Early Education* London: Paul Chapman (second edition)

Onyefulu, I. (2005) *Chidi Only Likes Blue: an African Book of Colours* London: Frances Lincoln Ltd.

Ouvry, M. (2003) *Exercising Muscles and Minds* London: National Children's Bureau

Pachter, C. (2008) *M is for Moose* Canada: Cormorant

Paley, V. G. (1984) *Boys and Girls: Superheroes in the Doll Corner* Chicago: University of Chicago Press

Paley, V. G. (1987) *Wally's Stories Conversations in the Kindergarten* Cambridge MA: Harvard University Press

Paley, V. G. (2014) *The Kindness of Children* Cambridge MA: Harvard University Press Chicago Press

Paley, V.G. (2000) *White Teacher* Cambridge MA: Harvard University Press

Paton Walsh, J. (1993) *When Grandma Came* London: Puffin

Peter, S. (2003) *Tree of Life* London: Walker Books

Petty, K. and Maizels, J. (1999) *The Magnificent I Can Read Music Book* London: Random House Children's Books

Petty, K. and Maizels, J. (2000*) The Wonderful World Book* London: Random House

Piaget, J. (2002) *The Language and Thought of the Child* London: Routledge Classic (first published in Paris, 1923)

Piaget, J. (2013) *Play, Dreams and Imitation in Childhood* London: Routledge (first published 1951)

Pike, N. (1983) *The Peach Tree* New York: Stemmer House Publishers

Pirrie, J. (1987) *On Common Ground: a programme for teaching poetry* London: Hodder and Stoughton

Pratt, C. (1990) *I Learn from Children: An Adventure in Progressive Education* London: Harpercollins (first published 1948)

Puttock, S. (2001) *A Ladder to the Stars* London: Frances Lincoln Ltd.

Quentin, B. (2012) *Quentin Blake's ABC* London: Red Fox

Ransome, A. (2012) *Swallows and Amazons* London: Vintage (first published 1930)

Ray, J. (1997) *Hansel and Gretel* London: Walker Books

Ray, J. (2004) *Adam and Eve and the Garden of Eden* London: An Eden Project Book

Ray, J. (2009) *Snow White: a three dimensional fairy tale theatre* London: Walker Books

Reggio Children (1996) *City in the Rain* in Catalogue of the Hundred Languages of Children Exhibition, Reggio Emilia: Reggio Children

Reggio Children (1996) *From a Puddle* in Catalogue of the Hundred Languages of Children Exhibition, Reggio Emilia: Reggio Children

Reggio Children (1997) *Shoe and Metre* Reggio Emilia: Reggio Children

Rich, D. Drummond, M.J. and Myer, C. (2008) *Learning: what matters to children* Woodbridge: Rich Learning Opportunities

Richardson, R. (2002) *In Praise of Teachers* Stoke on Trent: Trentham Books

Rinaldi, C. (2006) *In Dialogue with Reggio Emilia: listening, researching and learning* London: Routledge

Ringgold, F. (1996) *Tar Beach* New York: Dragonfly Books

Roberts, D. and MacDonald, A. (2012) *Dirty Bertie: Pirate* London: Stripes

Roberts, R. (ed.)(2001) *PEEP Voices: a Five Year Diary* Oxford: PEEP

Robinson, M. (2006) *Kandinsky* London: Flame Tree Publishing

Rosen, M. (2000) *We're Going on a Bear Hunt* London: Walker Books Ltd.

Rosen, M. (2013) *Alphabetical: how every letter tells a story* London: John Murray

Sachar, L. (2000) *Holes* London: Bloomsbury

Saramago, J. (2013) *Blindness.* London: Vintage Books First published in Portugal in 1995. See also *Seeing* (2004)

Say, A. (1991) *Tree of Cranes* New York: Houghton Mifflin Company

Schattschneider D and Walker, W. (1978) *MC Escher Kaleidocycles* Norfolk: Tarquin Publications

Schiller, C. (1979) in Griffin Beale, C.(ed) *Christian Schiller in his Own Words* London: A. and C. Black

Schweitzer, S. (2006) *Well I Wonder* Forest Row: Sophia Books

Selznick, B. (2011) *The Invention of Hugo Cabret* London: Scholastic

Sendak, M (1996) *In the Night Kitchen* New York: Harper Collins

Sendak, M. (1986) *The Sign on Rosie's Door* London: Puffin

Sewel, A. (2014) *Black Beauty* London: Puffin Chalk (first published 1877)

Sheldon. D. (1995) *The Garden* London: Red Fox

Simon, N. (1995) *Wet World* London: Walker Books Ltd.

Sis, P. (1993) *The Tree of Life: Charles Darwin* London: Walker Books Ltd.

Smith, L. (2011) *It's a Book* London: Macmillan Children's Books

Sophocles (1990) *The Cure at Troy*, in Philoctetes translated by Seamus Heaney London: Faber and Faber

Speed Shaskan, T. (2012) *Honestly, Red Riding Hood was Rotten! The story of Little Red Riding Hood as told by the wolf* London: Puffin, Picture Window Books

Stojic, M. (2000) *Rain* London: David Bennett Books Ltd.

Storm, R. (2014) *The Astrological Zodiac for Children* Atglen, PA: Schiffer Publishing Ltd.

Tanner, R. (1987) *Double Harness* Bath: Impact Books Ltd.

Thomson, B. (2013) *Fossil* Seattle: Two Lions

Tilman, N. (2005) *On the Night You Were Born* Oregon: Darling Press

Tolkien, J.R.R. (2013) *The Hobbit: Illustrated Edition* London: HarperCollins (first published 1937)

Tolstoy, A. (1989) *The Great Big, Enormous Turnip* London: Mammoth

Tomlinson, J. (2014) *The Owl Who Was Afraid of the Dark* London: Egmont

Tomlinson, T. (1997) *Little Stowaway* London: Jonathan Cape

Traditional *Little Red Riding Hood*

Traditional *The Princess and the Pea*

Traditional *The Three Bears*

Troupe, T.K. (2012) *The Story of Cassiopeia: a Roman Constellation* Mankato, Minnesota: Capstone Press

Tucker, K. (2001) *Do Knights Take Naps?* London: Cat's Whiskers

Twain, M. (2010) *The Adventures of Huckleberry Finn* London: Collins (first published 1885)

Venezia, M. (2008) *Getting to Know the World's Greatest Artists: Faith Ringgold* New York: Scholastic Children's Press

Vernon Lord, J. (1988) *The Giant Jam Sandwich* London: Macmillan

Voake, C. (2007) *A Little Guide to Wildflowers:* Eden Project Books London: Random House

Voake, C. (2011) *A Little Guide to Trees:* Eden Project Books London: Random House

Waddell, M. (1996) *The Big Big Sea* London: Walker Books

White, E.B. (2003) *Charlotte's Web* London: Puffin (first published (1952)

Wilenski, D. (2014) *A Story of Smallness and Light* Cambridge: Cambridge Curiosity and Imagination

Wilenski, D. and Wending, C. (2013) *Fantastical Guides for the Wildly Curious: Ways into Hinchingbrooke Country Park* Cambridge: Cambridge Curiosity and Imagination

Williams, M. (2006) *The Iliad and the Odyssey* London: Walker Books

Williams, M. (2007) *The Velveteen Rabbit* London: Egmont

Williams, M. (2010) *King Arthur and the Knights of the Round Table* London: Walker Books

Wilson, E. (1988) *Islamic Designs* London: British Museum Press

Winterson, J. (2013) *Why We Need Fairy Stories*: Jeanette Winterson on Oscar Wilde's Fairy Tales in The Guardian newspaper, 13th October 2013

Wormwell, C. (2002) *The New Alphabet of Animals* London: Running Press

Young, J. (1990) *A Million Chameleons* Boston, MA: Little, Brown and Company

Yousafzai, M. (2013) *I am Malala: the girl who stood up for education and was shot by the Taliban* London: Weidelfield and Nicholson

Poems

de la Mare, W. (1962) *The Listeners* in de la Mare Poems by Walter de la Mare. London: Puffin

Donaldson, J. (2013) *The Further Adventures of the Owl and the Pussy-Cat* London: Puffin Books

Drinkwater, J. (2006) *Moonlit Apples*, in Barefoot Book of Classic Poems ed. Jackie Morris Cambridge MA: Barefoot Books

Foster, J. and Paul, K. (2004) *Monster Poems* Oxford: Oxford University Press

Harrison, M. (1988) *The Blue Room* in Edwards, R. Oxford: Oxford University Press

Harrison, M. (1988) *The Greater Cats* Sackville-West, V. Oxford: Oxford University Press

Harvey, A, (1991) *Shades of Green* London: Random Century Group Ltd.

Holub, M. (1967) *The Door* in Milner, I. and Theiner, G. Selected Poems. London: Penguin

Hopkins, G. M (1969) *Pied Beauty* in Mackay, D. A Flock of Words. London: Bodley Head

Levertov, D. (2003) *O Taste and See in* New Selected Poems Northumberland: Bloodaxe Books

Longfellow, H.W. (1983) *Hiawatha* New York: Puffin Pied Piper Books

Morgan, E. (1981) *The Apple's Song in* McGough, R. Strictly Private. London: Viking Kestrel

Monro, H. (2003) *Overheard on a Saltmarsh* in Duffy, C.A. Overheard on a Saltmarsh: Poet's Favourite Poems. London: Young Picador

Morris, J. (2011) *The Cat and the Fiddle, a treasury of nursery rhymes* London: Frances Lincoln

Patten, B. (1999) *The Blue and Green Ark: an alphabet for planet Earth* London: Scholastic Children's Books

Prevert, J. (1964) *To Make a Portrait of a Bird* in Happenings: ed Wollman, M. and Grugeon, D. London: Harrap and Co.

Rosen, M. (ed.) (2009) *Classic Poetry an illustrated collection* London: Walker Books (first printed1998)

Siegen-Smith, N .(1999) *A Pocketful of Stars: poems about the night* Bristol: Barefoot Books Ltd.

Stevenson, R.L. (2008) Bed in Summer in A Child's Garden of Verses London: Puffin Books first published 1885

Traditional (1989) *The Key to the Kingdom* in Craft, R. The Song That Sings the Bird: Poems for Young Children. London: Collins Sons and Co Ltd.

Works of art

Boyle Family (1986) *Beyond Image* (Catalogue for the Boyle Family Exhibit) London: Arts Council of Great Britain

Brown, F.M. (1865) *The Last of England*, oil on panel, Birmingham: Birmingham Museum and Art Gallery

Brownlow, E. (1858) *The Foundling Restored to its Mother*, oil on canvas, London: The Foundling Museum

Brueghel, P. (1565) *Haymaking*, oil on panel, Prague: National Gallery

Fildes, L. (1887) *The Doctor*, oil on canvas, London: Tate Britain

Harnett, W. (1988) *My Gems*, oil on wood, Washington D.C.: National Gallery of Art

Hitchins, I. (1967) *White Sea Cloud,* oil on canvas

Nolde, E. (1930) *The Sea B*, oil on canvas, London: Tate Modern

Moss, A.and Wardley, J. (2013) *The Fallen 9000* www.sandinyoureye.co.uk

Peto, J. (1865) *Letter Rack,* oil on canvas, London: Tate Britain

Picasso, P. (1937) *Guernica*, oil on canvas, Madrid: Museo Reina Sofia

Pippin, H. (1946) *Victorian Interior*, oil on canvas, New York: Metropolitan Museum of Art

Ringgold, F. (1990) *Tar Beach II,* quilt, Virginia: Museum of Fine Art

Snape, W.H. (1891) *The Cottage Home*, oil on canvas,

Toyoharu, U. (circa mid 1770s) *Interior and Landscape*, woodcut, Washington D.C.: Freer Gallery

van Gogh, V. (1889) *The Starry Night,* oil on canvas, New York City: Museum of Modern Art

van Gogh, V. (1885) *The Potato Eaters* , oil on canvas, Amsterdam: Van Gogh Museum

Whistler, J.M. *Nocturne in Blue and Gold: Old Battersea Bridge*, oil paint, London: Tate Britain

Music

A Midsummer Night's Dream, Overture in E major (1826) Felix Mendelsohn

Bolero (1928) Joseph-Maurice Ravel

Carnival of the Animals (1886) Camille Saint-Saëns

Cats' Duet (1825) Gioachino Rossini (attributed)

Ghillie Callum or traditional Scottish Sword Dance

'Moonlight' Sonata, Piano Sonata no. 14 (1801) Ludwig van Beethoven

Mosquito Dance (1931) Béla Bartòk

Nocturnes (1782-1837) John Field

Peter Grimes (1945) Benjamin Britten

Prelude Opus 28, no. 15 'The Raindrop' (1838) Frédéric Chopin

Purple Haze (1967) Jimi Hendrix, The Jimi Hendrix Experience

Purple People Eater (1958) Sheb Wooley, MGM Records

Rhapsody in Blue (1924) George Gershwin

Romeo and Juliet (Dance of the Knights) (1935) Sergei Prokoviev

Singing in the Rain (1952) Arthur Freed and Nacio Herb Brown CD (1996)
     Rhino Records

Star Wars: A New Hope, Original Motion Picture Soundtrack (1997) John
     Williams, RCA

Starry Starry Night, 'Vincent' (1971) Don MacLean, United Artists Records

The Goldberg Variations (1741) Johann Sebastian Bach

The Monster Mash (1962) Bobby Boris Pickett, Universal Music

The 1812 Overture in Eb major, Op 49 (1880) Pieter Tchaikovsky

The Planets, Op. 32 (1914-1916) Gustav Holst

Vltava (1874) Bedřich Smetana

West Side Story (1957) Leonard Bernstein

Video and DVD

Singing in the Rain (2003) Production Warner Home Video DVD [3942-DV]

Every effort has been made to ensure that all references are accurate but if any are incorrect, the publishers will be pleased to make the necessary arrangements at the first opportunity.

Index